This book is dedicated to Jean Pascal Kapps.
Family. Friend.

HOW TO TEACH

Here endeth the lesson ...

THE BOOK OF
PLENARY

PHIL BEADLE

Independent Thinking Press

First published by

Independent Thinking Press
Crown Buildings, Bancyfelin, Carmarthen, Wales, SA33 5ND, UK
www.independentthinkingpress.com

Independent Thinking Press is an imprint of Crown House Publishing Ltd.

Extracts from *Visible Learning for Teachers: Maximising Impact on Learning (2012) and Visible Learning: A Synthesis of over 8200
Meta-Analyses Relating to Achievement* (2009) © John Hattie have been reprinted with the kind permission of Routledge.

Extract from Paul Dix, 'Stop Thinking That Your Objectives Interest Me' (2011) is available from http://www.pivotaleducation.
com/stop-thinking-that-your-objectives-interest-me/ and has been used with permission. www.pivotaleducation.com.

Extracts from *Think of a Link: How to Remember Absolutely Everything*, text copyright © Andy Salmon, 2011.
Reproduced by permission of Scholastic Ltd. All rights reserved.

British Library Cataloguing-in-Publication Data
A catalogue entry for this book is available
from the British Library.

Print ISBN 978-1-78135-053-9
Mobi ISBN 978-1-78135-072-0
ePub ISBN 978-1-78135-073-7

Printed and bound in the UK by
Gomer Press Llandysul, Ceredigion

ACKNOWLEDGEMENTS

It is now long overdue that I thank Caroline Lenton who, despite the evidence, is still of the belief that a book on education can be comic without necessarily making the writer a clown, and who sees some value in me. I'd also like to thank Rosalie Williams, for whom nothing is ever too much trouble. And I'd like to thank Bev Randell, who knows a silk purse when she sees one.

Thanks are also due to David Didau for casting an eye, and for providing competition worthy of the name.

CONTENTS

INTRODUCTION

G. K. Chesterton once wrote that he was 'too ready to write books on the feeblest provocation'.[1] It is reasonable to suggest that the existence of the transiently useful artefact you are now holding could be evidence that the same accusation could be levelled at its author.[2]

This book is an experiment to see if it is possible to make something – a thing that is (perhaps), by nature, intrinsically boring – in some way interesting. (This could reasonably be argued to be the mark of a decent teacher.) So, it is a challenge I have set myself: is it possible to spend a few months immersed in the shallow puddle of the plenary, and come out holding some form of brittle petal that will not only help you, dear colleague, to improve your practice, but will also entertain?

The process of writing this thin volume has been to read everything ever written about the plenary, and try to turn it into a series of workable jokes. And then, having failed to do so, to tell you about the best strategies, and how you might go about implementing them; as well as which ones you should avoid, because they are either stupid (see the anagram and the wordsearch), or because they are merely a marginal, incremental repetition of some non-idea (see both the anagram and, indeed, the wordsearch). But before we go into the useful arena of the practical and specific, let's briefly divert into a more 'big picture' look at the plenary.

---

1   G. K. Chesterton, *Orthodoxy* (Mineola, NY: Dover, 2004), 1.
2   As Alastair Smith brilliantly puts it: 'I like self-deprecating humour …
     I'm just not very good at it.'

By the end of this chapter (I hope) you will be able to:

1   Identify and articulate what your students will get out of a well-conducted plenary.

2   Regurgitate what Ofsted have to say about plenaries and, in particular, where they think we are going wrong.

3   Clarify what you think about certain aspects of planning a plenary (relating the plenary to the objectives, starting with a plenary, mini plenaries) – good or bad.

4   Relate to the problems that your students might have with plenaries, and have strategies to overcome these.

5   Use the plenary as an effective part of your already well-developed Assessment for Learning (AfL) strategies.

6   Relate your understanding of the plenary to what Professor John Hattie has to say about the end of the lesson.

7   Be marginally better read on the subject of domain specificity than your colleagues and, perhaps, have an opinion as to whether domain-general and domain-specific ideas of cognition are mutually exclusive or not. (This may not make any sense to you now. And it may not make any sense to you later on.)

And that's just Part 1.

Organisationally, the book has been constructed (if that is not too baroque a term for such a short tome) with in-built differentiation at its core. The majority of readers will want a brief overview of how one might most profitably conduct a plenary (this is in Part 1: An Overview of the Plenary), and a few decent ideas on easy strategies to use that may have some benefit for their students (this is in Part 2: Analogue Plenaries). If your needs have been fulfilled by these two sections, I'd advise you not to bother going any further, as the second half of this book is heavy going if you are not of a mind to try and understand some nearly difficult stuff.

For the gifted and talented reader(s) – teaching spods, bloggers, CPD coordinators and assistant and deputy heads in charge of teaching and learning – there is an acknowledgement that writing a book, however short, on a metacognitive activity and not brushing on metacognition would be an act of professional negligence (it is therefore covered, albeit clumsily, in Part 3: Metacognition for Beginners). Where the book begins to fly a little, and where it is, I feel, potentially useful is in Part 4: Digital Plenaries. Many of these ideas will appear, and indeed are, simple. I'd say that this is not necessarily a reason to write them off, as it is rarely simplicity that is the enemy in teaching. It is in this section that I have attempted to translate my reading of the research into strategies that, plausibly, might have a substantial impact on the students' learning in your specific domain.[3]

---

3   If you understand that this is a joke (albeit an unfunny one), then you should definitely read Parts 3 and 4.

PART 1
AN OVERVIEW OF
THE PLENARY

Firstly, let us acknowledge that the plenary is not in any way sexy; the word itself is unpleasingly under-erotic, seeming to bring to mind some unpalatable infection of the penis: *pleeenary*.

'What's wrong with it, Doctor?'

'Aside from the size? Well, sadly, I must inform you that you have a nasty little dose of non-specific plenary.'

And that, dear colleagues, may well be one of the reasons – go on, be honest – that you (or I) do not always do them. In fact, you can pretty well guarantee that if you get working parties together in schools to examine the assorted parts of our professional practice, and give various groups their pick of what they are going to look at, you'll find, at the end, that the plenary is sat parked, about as popular as a ginger stepson, as the last forlorn car in the garage.

There is also the added weirdness that the word 'plenary', to a teacher in the United Kingdom, signifies something that it doesn't mean to anyone else in sane society or the wider world. To people who inhabit workplaces devoid of staffrooms, a plenary is the compulsory bit of a conference when delegates all come back from the 'break-out' rooms or the workshops into the main hall. It is during a 'plenary' that you will most likely have to sit through a tedious 'keynote' speech from an academic or bore (or both).

Alternatively, if you are in (or of) the Church, you might think of it as a form of authority: the power a Church's governing body has to set out exactly what it is going to do. It is only in the British staffroom that we hear this word and think immediately, 'Oh, the ten-minute bit at the end of the lesson that I can never really be bothered to do properly (if at all)!'

The name came about, I think, because plenary is the adjectival version of the Latin noun, *plenum*, which does not even go so far as to exactly correspond to the concept of 'fullness': it merely carries a suggestion of it. The inference here is that in conducting a proper plenary we are giving our students the suggestion of fullness: which is an uncomfortable image, until we remind ourselves that the idea is to set students on the path to being replete with *learning*.

Another of the reasons that the plenary attracts a certain dwarfism of attention is that it's extremely difficult to get intellectually interested, or in any way passionate, about the question, 'So, children, what did you learn today?'

However, if we are to start off with the briefest analysis of what our students might (potentially) get out of a good plenary — and accepting that we all want to be the best teacher we can possibly be — then it becomes a professional dictate (perhaps) that we start taking them seriously and devoting a little imagination and thought to their use, or their implementation, or their management, or their whatever.

WHAT WILL YOUR STUDENTS GET OUT OF A GOOD PLENARY?

'What's the point of all this stopping ten minutes before the end of the lesson and then doing some weirdness, Sir, just when we've understood what you wanted us to do in the main task?' Could Denzil be right here? What's the point? The lesson is going swimmingly. Why stop it, and manage yet another oh-so-bloody-knackering-and-difficult transition, just at the exact part of the lesson at which you are most tired?

Alternatively, what's the point? The lesson has been a disaster from start to finish; the kids have been fractious all along.[4] Why stop it, and manage yet another oh-so-difficult transition, just at the point when you are most tired?

Look at it through another similarly phrased prism: what's the point? What's the point of going to all that trouble planning an interesting sequence of activities and inputs when they don't remember anything from the lesson? You may just as well have got them to do some lovely colouring-in (!). What's the point of going all the way to 85% and just throwing the last 15% in the waste-bin? What's the point of having thought really hard about the content of the lesson and then copped out just at the bit where they actually cement the information in their heads? What's the point of painting something if you aren't going to varnish it? The colour will all wash off come the first passing shower.

Without the plenary you are arguably just going through the motions and passing time. It was a nice enough experience, but they don't remember it. And the point of lessons is that they are remembered, otherwise they are not lessons learnt.

---

4   'Sir looks a bit grey today. Let's mess about!'

The existence of the plenary is to help the students remember what they have learnt in the lesson. If you don't, erm, *do one* it is vastly more than likely that they will have substantially less recall of the learning. If we shift the focus to Professor John Hattie, he's quite categorical:

> The lesson does not end when the bell goes. It ends when teachers interpret the evidence of their impact on student(s) during the lessons relative to their intended learning outcomes and initial criteria of success – that is when teachers review the learning through the eyes of their students.[5]

There are a few elements to this observation that benefit from a brief unpacking. Firstly, Hattie here gives implicit, yet emphatic, confirmation that some checking of the learning must take place; the end of the lesson seems a quite reasonable place at which to do this. Secondly, he is explicit that we've somehow to reframe the way that we look at the learning experience so that it is the opinion(s) of the students that lead us to review and alter what we are doing in lessons. (There is a pro forma that will be of help if you want to take Hattie's observation as being the gospel here, in the first of the digital plenaries in Part 4: Homework's Holy Grail.)

In performing a task that is specifically related to the learning (and to the objectives), students may come to new realisations and make new connections they hadn't made earlier on in the lesson. Consequently, a decent plenary will extend and broaden their knowledge of the concept or skill being taught.

However, there is also a quite interesting and entirely reasonable argument that the best thing students will get out of a decent plenary is an understanding of what they do not know. As Darren Mead, whose Pedagogical

---

5   John Hattie, *Visible Learning for Teachers: Maximising Impact on Learning* (Abingdon: Routledge, 2012), 145.

Purposes blog reveals him to be perhaps the most intellectually engaged of all British teachers, states: 'Becoming less confident in their knowledge is just as valid a response, as they could either be unlearning a misconception, which is a difficult process or be questioning why they believe something rather just accepting something is right.'[6]

Mead is bang on here, and his assertion tallies nicely with Hattie's thoughts (above) about the same: specifically, that what we should be looking for is for the students to be able to identify what they don't understand and to implement (practised) strategies to obtain that knowledge; to fill that gap.

WHAT DOES MR LESSON INSPECTOR SAY?

Here's what those who are employed to take out kitchen scales from shiny briefcases and comment on the weight of a thing had to say about our use of plenaries some considerable time ago.[7] Ofsted's evaluation of the Key Stage 3 pilot in English and maths commented that teachers are good at standing at the front of classrooms reading lesson objectives to our students from a PowerPoint, and that we're also good at giving the students a pointless activity that takes ten minutes at the beginning of a lesson. They are less happy, however, with the plenary; and pointedly use the language 'lack of well managed' and 'weakness' in a rather unpleasantly pointed manner:

---

6   Darren Mead, 'Metacognitive Wrappers' (2010). Available at http://pedagogicalpurposes. blogspot.co.uk/2010/11/metacognitive-wrappers.html (accessed 22 May 2013).

7   And I mean, ages. There is very little analytical thought that has been published on the plenary, which is why this book is already the seminal text on it: no one else could be bothered to write one.

The plenary is an essential part of the lesson, but its quality has not improved since the strategy began. This is a matter of serious concern. As with independent work, part of the problem lies in a lack of understanding of its purposes; for assessment, feedback, consolidation, evaluation and the linking of the lesson to the next one, or to another area of the curriculum.[8] The plenary is poorly used if it is simply a bolt-on-extra which provides an opportunity for groups of pupils to present their work daily; it is essential time for making sure that pupils have grasped the objectives and made progress, so that the next lesson can begin on firm foundations.[9]

Broadly, the problem with the plenary session, as it is currently (or was previously) used in British education, is that they are (or were) not performed with enough seriousness of intent: we tend to just go through the motions when we are being observed and, even then, don't devote anything like enough time to it. Ofsted go on:[10]

From the outset, plenaries were often the weakest part of the lesson. Good planning was critical to the success of plenaries. Often there was insufficient time for them, typically because teachers underestimated the time required for activities in the main phase of the lesson. Plenaries were often the least active part of lessons. Teachers tended merely to sum up what happened during the main phase and pupils did not have the opportunity to articulate what they had learned. When pupils had such opportunities, they proved an important part of the learning process.[11]

---

8   See Part 2, Plenary 6 (Extended Abstraction) for why this idea is rubbish.

9   Ofsted, *The National Literacy Strategy: The Third Year*. Ref: 332 (London: Ofsted, 2001). Available at: http://www.ofsted.gov.uk/resources/national-literacy-strategy-third-year (accessed 22 May 2013), 54.

10   Don't they?

11   Ofsted, *The Key Stage 3 Strategy: Evaluation of the First Year of the Pilot*. Ref: 349 (London: Ofsted, 2002). Available at: http://dera.ioe.ac.uk/16531/ (accessed 22 May 2013), 11.

If we reverse the box tickers' conclusions as to why plenaries are poor, we can state fairly conclusively what the fundamentals of a good one would be.

1 **It has to be planned**

You can't just go into a lesson with any sense that you will just pull something out of the bottomless well of your imagination. With all the will in the world, if you think you can just magic one up from nowhere, you are kidding yourself and in forty minutes' time you will be asking them, 'So what did you learn in this lesson?' You'll go into the lesson intent on finding a little moment in which you can rustle up an idea, but you'll get caught up in something else. Keith will require some tissues for his bottom lip. Everyone will want your attention. You will forget.

2 **You have to leave sufficient time for them**

Key to this is not to see plenaries as the end of the lesson, but as an intrinsic part of it. What tends to happen is that teachers get caught up in the main lesson activity, as they (not unreasonably) give the 'body' of the lesson due preference. This has its head on the wrong way round. It is the mindset of seeing the plenary as a tacked-on irrelevance that makes the majority of them ineffective; they should be seen not as a tacked-on imposition, but as a vital part of the lesson's function. There's no point whatsoever in teaching good lessons that bring in sparkling and vital new knowledge if the kids have forgotten that information before they have even got as far as the classroom door. So, fundamental to running a decent plenary is to give it a decent fist of time. Ten minutes, not two.[12] This will also ensure that,

---

12 There is a school of thought, however, that thinks the plenary can be of variable length: two minutes on a Monday, twenty on a Tuesday, thirteen-and-a-half on a Friday. It's not unreasonable. However, the key here is that you plan for it, and that in planning you leave a reasonable amount of time for a planned activity.

as you have to fill a full, fat chunk of time, you avoid the other key sin: which is not having them active enough!

3 **Get the kids to do the work!**

In the olden days, when the plenary was but a whelp, the guidance was simple: the kids got their coats on, and before they left the class the teacher asked them what they had learnt. They came up with a few listless replies, because they already had their coats on and they were already somewhere else altogether in their minds. When they did reply they would come up with completely the wrong answer, and would make the teacher look like a berk if that teacher was being observed by the men-in-black. You thought you had taught them some immensely technical and simultaneously spiritual concept and skill. They would reply: 'I learnt it is proper good to be friendly to uvver peepul, innit,' or that 'Racism is double naughty.' An unsatisfactory game all round.

Ofsted's suggestion here is that, certainly at the time the report was written, even standing at the front and asking kids what they had learnt wasn't happening. The implication is that in the early days most plenaries consisted of the teacher standing at the front of the class telling them what they had covered. This practice lets the teacher tick a box on the lesson plan that says they have done/performed/what-evered a plenary, but it isn't in any way a cognitive act for the pupils.

If one takes the orthodox viewpoint that students learn more when they are actively engaged in a task that they perform themselves, then it stands to reason that a plenary which involves the teacher telling them stuff that he or she has already told them is a plenary that is not effective in terms of sticking the information from the lesson in the head you want it stuck in.

In short then, of the three options – designing a specific plenary task for them to do, asking them what they have learnt and telling them what you've taught them – the former is clearly the best, but if you are going to just tack a plenary on, it is better to ask them what they have learnt than to sum up.

Another thing that will get you a grudging 'needs improvement' from the career weasels is getting kids to present their work at the end of the lesson. Let's be honest here: it's a complete waste of time. Kids stand at the front in groups of four, only one person says anything, and all that person actually does is monotonously intone a bare sentence comprised of spartan, frigid words that have been hastily scribbled onto a folded piece of lined A4. Everyone else just stands looking like a spare part doing the embarrassed side-together-side-together crab shuffle, desperately wishing their un-longed for moment in this dimmest of spotlights ends, soon, please, soon. No one learns anything, but we have 'presented' our work. (If you must do this – and don't – then ban students from having any form of script and forbid them from learning allocated lines off pat. Then enter into a reasoned analysis of either their learning – 'What did this group learn that you didn't know?' – or get the viewing students to be critical, in a positive and constructive way, of the way in which it was presented.)

KEY SKILLS IN PLANNING: RELATE THE PLENARY TO THE OBJECTIVES

As should be obvious, there must be a relationship between the plenary and the objectives. As the plenary is an attempt to ensure that what we have said we are going to learn has been learnt and – crucially – retained, then, when planning a lesson, one might argue that *the plenary and objectives should be planned at more or less exactly the same time*, in that one must necessarily influence the other.

However, whilst it is easy to see how the plenary would be influenced by the objectives, it is perhaps a greater intellectual leap to conceive of how the opposite might apply. An explanation: one of the bigger issues with effective plenaries is the problem of when they are tacked on to a lesson which has too broad or too scattergun an approach to the notion of there being discrete, identifiable things to be learnt in the lesson. Where the objectives are too diffuse, where there are too many of them, where they are not tight enough or where they are focused on something too vaporous to be either identifiably something that can be learnt or something that is of any value to the learner, it becomes impossible to run an effective plenary. You cannot properly consolidate the knowledge, skills or understanding when that knowledge, skills or understanding has been ill defined at the front end of the lesson or absent during it.

I have previously been sceptical about the process of sharing lesson objectives with students.[13] But people develop their ideas (about) and understanding(s) of things, and I've changed my mind. During a whole summer 12,000 miles away from my family, teaching in a school in Australia, I witnessed the unintended consequences of a school system that does not stipulate that teachers tell the students what they are going to learn at the beginning of the lesson. And that is: when you ask the students what they are learning in a lesson, they look at you as if you have farted at their mothers! If you don't tell students what they are going to learn, they are unable to articulate what they are learning (unless they are very bright indeed).

This raises an interesting philosophical diversion which, if you have the time to spare, is worth considering for a second or two: if you can't articulate what you are learning, then are you learning it? The answer is not necessarily obvious and, moreover, not necessarily the one at which you might initially grasp. But it does tend to lead one in the direction of concluding

---

13 If you are remotely interested then there is an article about what I thought about them in 2007 at http://www.guardian.co.uk/education/2007/jan/16/schools.uk1/.

that if having the learning intentions stated at the beginning of the lesson helps students to articulate what they are learning in a lesson, then it seems churlish to withhold that information from them. (Unless, of course, you are breaking the rules deliberately and with intent.)

In terms of the relationship between the objectives and the plenary, whilst the former defines the learning intended, the latter must get to the heart of the learning and decide whether it has taken place or not. Consequently, the heart of the learning must be evident to the teacher. It is less than ideal just throwing a further, final task at the students that is somehow related to the subject of the learning when it is not focused on the specific learning intentions that were stated at the outset. The correct intentions here can be summed up in the kind of crass rhyming aphorism that features in many a dull-as-ditchwater teacher-training day: in planning the perfect plenary, you should be – theoretically, at least – seeking to obtain 'consolidation not rela- tion'. The temptation, when you are performing an active plenary, can be to just throw an activity at it, which doesn't necessarily involve analysing the learning that has taken place (or not) in the lesson. In this way we fill the ten minutes pleasingly enough, but we ignore the plenary's chief function, which is to consolidate the knowledge acquired over the last hour.

KEY ISSUES IN PLANNING: SHARING THE PLENARY EARLY DOORS

On a related topic, many teachers use the sharing of objectives as a point at which they also share the plenary (this is a particularly useful technique when you are being observed, and you know damn well the observer is only going to see out the cursory first twenty minutes, and has no intention whatsoever of being around for the plenary). Many teachers, keen to display that thought has gone into the bit of the lesson that the observer is unlikely to see, and equally keen to ensure that students have their ears pricked so they might perform well in the test at the end of the lesson, share the questions that they will be asking: 'At the end of the lesson, I will be asking you the following questions, and I will be expecting you to know the answers!' Some use this technique in tandem with sharing the objectives; some, even more cleverly, replace the objectives entirely with this technique, as their sharing is inferred, or is implicit, within the process of asking or answering the questions. If you can answer the questions at the end of the lesson, you will have achieved the objectives. It doesn't matter that you haven't actually read them at the children.

KEY ISSUES IN PLANNING: MINI PLENARIES AND SHOWING PROGRESS

There is a shoal of thought that teachers should actually conduct more than just the one plenary in a lesson: that they should stop the lesson at various points to check understanding and to consolidate the learning gains. Some teachers start lessons with the statement, 'In twenty minutes I am going to ask you a question about how we factor quadratic equations. You will need to be ready with the answer.' And then, sure enough, in twenty minutes they do exactly what they said they were going to do. Some even go so far as asking students, at this point, to define what else it is they feel they need to know.

This all seems entirely logical. You get to a defined point somewhere along the continuum of the lesson, and use this as a fulcrum from which you can clarify and remedy misconceptions. (Furthermore, in doing so you are able to show progress to anyone observing you teach; and as progress *within* lessons is continually promoted by SMT despite Ofsted making almost no mention of it, it is very much a favoured strategy for teachers being Ofsteded.) You can also use it as a catch-up point. If certain students are struggling you can use front-of-class teaching to redirect them or to redefine the task so that they are able to complete or understand it more easily. The mini plenary becomes a staging post, therefore, in which you all briefly come together again, check where you are and then move on to the next bit.

It all seems perfectly reasonable, but there is a cogent counter-argument that in conducting mini plenaries we are reaching the empirical point of absolute absurdity – the tail-wagging-the-dog-which-has-a-face-where-its-bum-should-be-and-vice-versa – of a profession running everything so that they can please the inspectorate. Mini plenaries are the ultimate in, 'Look, for God's sake, you're trying so hard to please everyone else that you are losing sight of your own sanity', and their existence is causing even the bottom inspectorate to laugh at us. We are so desperate to show observers that our students are not only progressing over the year, but within individual lessons, and in the reductive absurdity of the reporting on the thing becoming more important than the thing itself, within miniscule tranches of that lesson.

A poster to the Learning Net Geography Forum site, who chooses to name him or herself 'Blue Square Thing', comes up with an elegant solution to the problem that in some ways also serves to encapsulate it.

> You have a grid … which does the old what do you know/now read the first bit of material – what do you now know/now do some research (or do the rest of the work) – now what do you know/now write x questions you want to find the answers out for.

This just sits on the desk and they fill it in every now and again – mini plenary time? It sort of shows progress in a way that even the most dull witted Ofsted dude can't fail to miss.[14]

Pedagogically, this idea is actually of some merit, though Jeff Huang (see Part 3) has shown that in terms of measuring the effect size of self-questioning, there is a slightly bigger effect if we do it before the lesson than after, and, crucially, that it is vastly lower if we do it during the lesson. So we can trot out the hoary old cliché, and conclude that research suggests mini plenaries are less effective than 'proper' end-of-lesson plenaries. As Darren Mead acknowledges, this makes sense: 'Common sense would suggest that trying to be self questioning during a lesson could be distracting to all but the most able learners.'[15]

I'd argue that it is the intent of the mini plenary, which is clearly to be noticed by the 'dull witted Ofsted dude' that makes them (whilst not pointless) something you might want to ask questions of or about. Much of the idea of the mini plenary seems to be orientated around this intent: to show progress, not over time, not over the space of a lesson, but over the space of a five-minute activity. Here we are in the region of appointing our favourite horse to be senator. If the intention of the mini plenary is to show to an outside observer – who visits the school once every four years – that our students are making progress over micro moments, then the profession is in a state where, perhaps, it needs to have a serious think about whether it is expending an inappropriate amount of time and effort on running everything in the classroom for distant and unloved relatives who visit only once every few years.

---

14 Available at http://learningnet.co.uk/geoforum/index.php?topic=5278.0 (accessed 22 May 2013).
15 Mead, 'Metacognitive Wrappers'.

Deputy head Keven Bartle, who writes a blog named, rather imaginatively, 'kevenbartle's Blog', is in agreement here, pointing out that Ofsted do not actually insist on progress within lessons:

> Much to our shame, even Ofsted (the big organisation but sadly not always the individual inspectors or inspection teams) realise that 'progress' is simply a numerical measurement of the distance between a start point and an end point and therefore *cannot in itself be observed in lessons* other than through assessing how much students have learned. 'Progress in lessons' is the very definition of a black box into which we, as teachers and leaders, need to shine a light.[16]

He is right to point out that even the guardians of conformity themselves think that progress within lessons is perhaps a little stupid as an idea: the people we are desperately trying to please are displeased at our attempts at pleasing them. The recent report from Ofsted Towers, entitled *Moving English Forward*, makes interesting reference to the same:

> In lessons observed, significant periods of time were spent by teachers on getting pupils to articulate their learning, even where this limited their time to complete activities and thereby interrupted their learning! Pupils need time to complete something before they can valuably discuss and evaluate it. To invite self- or peer-evaluation before pupils have had time to engage fully with learning is counter-productive.[17]

---

16   Keven Bartle, 'The Myth of Progress within Lessons' (2013). Available at http://dailygenius.wordpress.com/2013/02/12/the-myth-of-progress-within-lessons/ (accessed 22 May 2013), emphasis in original.

17   Ofsted (2012) *Moving English Forward*. Ref: 110118 (London: Ofsted). Available at: http://www.ofsted.gov.uk/resources/moving-english-forward (accessed 22 May 2013), 14.

So, whilst the inspectors are not saying that you definitely shouldn't conduct mini plenaries, they are suggesting that some teachers are going somewhat over the top in collecting what has been learnt before anything has, in fact, been learnt at all. In terms of your relationship with the plenary, or its diminutive brother, do remember not to put the horse before the cart: the kids have to learn something before they can go through the process of articulating what they have learnt.

Behaviour expert Paul Dix, lead trainer with Pivotal Education, chucks his oar in on a related subject with characteristic passion and aplomb:

> The inspectorate demands that 'learning is demonstrable' in 30/45 minutes and this lies in conflict with what we know about learning. Learning is more than good recall in the plenary. It is not proven by using the right key word at the right time or parroting the objectives back. It is not linear, predictable or even fully understood. It is wrong to encourage the notion that we can have control over when and how children learn. The honesty is taken out of what is happening. Teaching is reduced to absolutes, 'This is what you will learn in the next 30 minutes'. Pretending that we have control over learning is leading us further down the dark data driven, utterly accountable, unified methods path. Beware the 'units of learning' trolls who guard the bridge. They will try and convince you that all learning is quantifiable. They will take your soul and replace it with 'competences' without flinching.[18]

There is a further and interesting twist on the plenary function in Jim Smith's *Whole School Progress the Lazy Way: Follow Me, I'm Right Behind You*. In a serious, near-academic treatise, Jim lists four versions of progress checking (which is a major function of the plenary) and grades these from 'unsatisfactory'

---

18 Paul Dix, 'Stop Thinking That Your Objectives Interest Me' (2011). Available at http://www. pivotaleducation.com/stop-thinking-that-your-objectives-interest-me/ (accessed 22 May 2013).

to 'outstanding'. He satirises 'unsatisfactory' progress checking as, 'The old three-part lesson whereby the progress check (aka the plenary) came at the end of the lesson and with one minute to go it became apparent that nothing had been learnt and they were now yet another lesson nearer to being able to declare the whole year a write off.'[19] For Jim, progress checking (part of the 'aka the plenary' function) is a holistic circular process, which takes a while to get right. For Jim, the point of the plenary function is to alter learning behaviours and to lead in the direction of students being in a continual process of monitoring their own learning and behaviour for learning: 'Tasks are blended into the students' learning as opposed to the teacher's teaching. The task becomes invisible and develops into more of a learning-coaching conversation or an internal dialogue within each individual learner.'[20]

Jim's is a philosophically rich, intellectually diverting and profoundly modern approach, which is entirely in keeping with all the research on metacognition. He characterises the learning in which outstanding progress takes place as being 'realigned as a result of self, peer-to-peer or teacher led progress checks' and implicitly therefore takes a stand for a metacognitive form of in-lesson AfL that goes far beyond the glib notion of a mini plenary. But Jim's way takes a huge shift of thought and, for a supposedly 'lazy' strategy, potentially a bloody enormous amount of planning. It's worth engaging with the above quote, however, and asking yourself how you might implement this. What might it look like in reality?

---

19   Jim Smith, *Whole School Progress the Lazy Way: Follow Me, I'm Right Behind You* (Carmarthen: Crown House, 2012), 10.

20   Smith, *Whole School Progress the Lazy Way*, 12.

PUPILS' PROBLEMS WITH PLENARIES

There is a danger, since you are probably the only teacher in your school who is sufficiently interested in your own professional development to spend £12.99 on a book about the driest of all parts of teaching, that you will be the only teacher in the school who does them properly. This is OK in a functional environment – your class, your rules – but in less functional schools you may well be fighting an anti-achievement culture that the students have caught from *somewhere*, and instituting a regular plenary in every lesson will be perceived by some students as maverick behaviour on the part of the teacher, and so they will not take them seriously. Students are generally aware that the lesson should have some form of recap at the end, and are also aware that this, somehow, is the 'proper' way of doing things; but if, culturally, it is not entrenched as a professional expectation at your school, then you may be fighting a rising tide of negative opinion.

One of the key issues with pupils' responses, particularly if the plenary is a predominantly oral communication of learning, is that they can be wildly inaccurate about what they have learnt, coming up with absurdly esoteric responses so that they appear to be engaging with what teacher expects of them. Alternatively, you will often find that they are, in the initial stages of setting this as a lesson-by-lesson expectation, also massively inarticulate. Responses such as, 'I learnt that I don't like working with Shavonne' or 'I have learnt that English can be fun' are a fist of an attempt, but are not to be taken as a suggestion that learning of any depth or value has taken place.

Where responses are inarticulate or, worse still, uncomprehending and mute, or where responses misunderstand the point of the plenary, then there are ways of resolving this. The best is to appoint talk partners – to conduct an initial discussion of what has been learnt, either in pairs, threes or fours – and from then to throw it open to the appointed representatives of these groups.

One of the conclusions Paul Black and Dylan Wiliam[21] came to when they were looking at every piece of research ever undertaken into questioning in the classroom was that teachers are often happy with the immediate response of a student, and expected it immediately too. If you think how you might respond yourself if a figure of authority, perhaps after a day of mind-crushingly boring continuing professional development, asks you what you have learnt, and expects a (non-sarcastic) answer on the spot, in front of loads of your peers, you might begin to imagine the poor student's quandary when presented with this as a reasonable expectation by the teacher. They are expected to say something and, what is more, they are expected to say it *right now!* You haven't given them any time to think of what a rationalised and decently articulated response might be, and so they grasp blindly in the direction of a series of words that they hope might make sense.

Better to give them some time before they come up with a response, and to ensure that since this thinking time is in a group, that you are not asking Ali, who arrived last week from Pakistan, what he has learnt, when the only learning of any substance he has acquired since attending the school is the phrase 'fucking hell'.

The group will negotiate consensus as to what it is they think they have learnt, and will negotiate this consensus in language. Consequently, by giving them some time to come up with the answer it is likely that when it is delivered, as it has been discussed, it will be in as articulate and thoughtful a manner as they are capable of mustering.

An interesting idea here is to chunk down the ten minutes, so that you give three minutes thinking time in groups, a couple of minutes collecting these ideas – during which the teacher collects, reframes, rephrases and asks further questions about the learning – and then a further two minutes to

---

21 Paul Black and Dylan Wiliam, *Inside the Black Box: Raising Standards through Classroom Assessment* (London: GL Assessment, 1990).

go back to the groups and play with the ideas they have heard or the questions the teacher has raised. This all builds up into a final three minutes in whole-class mode, where the teacher can prove categorically that they have not taken the first thought as being the best thought: 'So, what we set out to learn today was … But what we really learnt was … Perhaps we need to revisit this subject again tomorrow.'

PLENARIES AS A FORM OF AFL

Clearly, when students are discussing or consolidating what (or indeed whether) they have learnt (anything) in the lesson, this is a key assessment point, and it is equally clear whatever assessment you've conducted can be used to plan the next lesson.

In its earliest days the plenary was intended as a point to 'link up' the learning; to allow students to see where they were in the gradational process of getting things into their heads. A key point of the plenary would be not only to remind the students of where they have just been, but to let them know where they were going next (which, of course, we never really knew, because we didn't actually have schemes of work as the head of department was completely overworked/a bit of a lazy bugger). The intention here was also to sell the next lesson, stimulating engagement and curiosity about the next step in the scheme of work and simultaneously letting them know there was a next step.

Currently, there is less of a dictate to use the plenary as a staging post in terms of letting children know they are on a continuum. It is, moreover, seen to be a point at which a teacher can assess whether the learning in the lesson has been successful. Here Dylan Wiliam and Paul Black's traffic light signals that students use to indicate whether they are secure (green), developing (orange) or nascent (red) in their understanding of a concept are amongst those most heavily approved of end-of-lesson techniques for the teacher who is interested in being saluted for proper adherence to last year's bloodless and unstylish gimmick handed down from academia for unquestioning conformists to adopt.

There are various derivations of this technique in use around British schools, from the coloured plastic cups used by Wiliam on BBC2's *The Classroom Experiment* (in which students were required to place the coloured cup indicating their perceived level of their own understanding over the top of the other two: bland, pedagogic Russian dolls), to students holding up cards to the teacher to indicate the same. (These come with the added joy for students of being able to show a much-disliked teacher the red card for every single thing they do.) Many schools include the cards as sections of the student planner so that they rarely, if ever, present any logistical issues in terms of being lost or in the amount of time a teacher has to waste distributing them.

One actually quite brilliant suggestion, which is made in *Working Inside the Black Box*, is that having asked the students to demonstrate their level of understanding at the beginning of the plenary, you then pair or group those who have chosen 'green' to demonstrate their confidence in their learning with those who have selected 'amber', so that the confident may teach the developing, whilst the teacher sits with the nascent – those who have understood little – and goes through it all once again.[22]

One might argue that, with the exception of the technique above, using the plenary to be diagnostic about individual learning needs is not entirely practicable in an ever-turning world. Sure, you'll have the ability to write down that Dwayne Dibbley doesn't understand quadratic equations, but you'll

---

22 Paul Black, Christine Harrison, Clare Lee, Bethan Marshall and Dylan Wiliam, *Working Inside the Black Box: Assessment for Learning in the Classroom* (Glasgow: Letts, 1990, 11).

invariably lose the piece of paper as soon as you've written his name on it. A more practical approach is using the plenary as an AfL task to inform your planning for the collective rather than the individual.

When not being observed, it is better to use such techniques to get a broader sense of the effectiveness (or not) of the lesson. It may be that with your teaching certificate and your fancy ways, you find a concept so pifflingly easy that you do not translate it well for your students, and they, consequently, find it confusing. The traffic light signals give a depersonalised insight into whether your students have actually learnt what you set out to do, and being in receipt of a slew of red cards or cups, you will know that you have to revisit that subject next lesson from a different slant or angle. (Or, alternatively, just repeat it in exactly the same manner again tomorrow, as the reason they 'didn't get it' is that they weren't listening.)

WHAT WOULD PROFESSOR HATTIE SAY?

A brave strategy for a plenary, which is something that perhaps you only attempt once you are established within the school, and if and when it is common knowledge amongst the students that you are a 'good' teacher, is asking them how the lesson went, and how they would go about improving it if we were to do it again. This is more a diagnostic, self-evaluative tool for your own development than it is a device with which to assess the learning of your students, but it will nevertheless give you some insights into not only their learning, but how you are doing with them. The danger in this gambit is that if it is deployed before there is a body of thought within the class that is decidedly pro-miss or pro-sir, it can give licence to rascals who just want to try on the coat of the naysayer. It can also give rise to the negative shrug, 'I just didn't like it'.

However, if you want to know anything about how lessons are going it is always best to ask a student: there is a chance that you will get some affirmation combined with a few comments that will change your practice for the better. Students are quite often the deepest thinkers about what is good or bad about the lesson they are in receipt of, and it is clearly a metacognitive task to ask students how their learning might be improved.

Fascinatingly, Professor Hattie seems to think that a process not dissimilar to this is actually something akin to the holy grail of teaching. He regards feedback from class to teacher as being of more actual significance than feedback from teacher to class. Another interesting point from Hattie's work (in terms of how it bounces up against metacognition) is the contention that our abilities at metacognitive regulation are not domain-independent, but are domain specific. In *Visible Learning*, he reports that metacognition must be taught mixed with each separate school subject, as most people find it hard to apply abstract rules in a wide variety of situations; people mostly work with more specific rules, which are situation-dependent. The corporate responsibility we all feel towards the education of the child is revealed by Hattie (to an extent, at least) to be a version of weeing into the wind. You will teach them these strategies thinking they will use them to advance their education in all of their lessons; they won't. These plenaries are just things they will use in your lesson. In the MFL lesson down the corridor, they will not be remembered or applied. *Quel dommage!*

However, it is worth having a look at whether this is actually true. Is metacognition domain general or domain specific?

A DIVERSION INTO DOMAINS: DOMAIN GENERAL/DOMAIN SPECIFIC

This is a debate from the academic study of reasoning that, in contrast to the assertions of many of those who comment on how education does or doesn't work, is actually entirely unresolved.

Broadly, the question is whether reasoning is a general set of skills that we apply in every area, or whether it is, in fact, specific to the area of reasoning. These polarities are classed by academics under two further distinct headings: domain general and domain specific. Domain-general knowledge might be contained in the answer to the question, 'How do I learn best?' Domain-specific would add the phrase, 'in geography' or 'with this spectacularly boring teacher'. By domain we mean the specific body of knowledge or subject area, not the space (though this is debatable according to the arguments for embedded cognition). If you think about your own particular strategies or skills, it is a fairly easy leap of thought to understand that perhaps our processes of cognition in working out a mathematical problem would be in some way distinct from working out a problem related to language; we will use distinct references and experiences to apply to the varying problems presented by the differing areas of study and perhaps also distinct areas of the brain. From here, it is not too much of a further leap to imagine that, if our cognition is distinct in these areas, then our metacognition might also be unique to content or context.

In the interests of cohesion, we'll briefly divert into the arguments for cognition being domain specific, and then examine whether it might be domain general.

ARGUMENTS FOR DOMAIN-SPECIFIC COGNITION: THE WASON TEST AND WHAT IT TELLS US

The Wason selection task is a reasoning test, the like of which the type of people who might be inclined to ascribe value to the completion of news-paper crosswords might enjoy. A series of cards with numbers and colours are set out and a series of unlucky human guinea pigs has to decide which one to turn over to provide a certain answer to a problem. (It's the kind of thing in which a spectacularly irritating and borderline autistic cousin might specialise.) What is of interest is that nearly everyone gets it wrong when the test sits within the realm of pure(ish) logic that is or has been disembodied from a specific context relating to life. It is only when the questions are con-textualised by being specific to a social issue – for instance, where you have to turn over the correct card to tell at what age a child might be allowed to drink sloe gin in a public house – that people start getting it right.

Weirdly, a further experiment that academics use to back up their claims for cognition being domain specific is related to simple addition and subtrac-tion. When asked to design the kind of maths problems you might encounter in the higher tier of a GCSE exam – 'Fred has got two apples. He eats one, then, being ecologically aware, he puts the core onto the compost heap. How many has he got left?' – and being given the option of making them addition or subtraction exercises, the context they were given affected the mathematical process they chose. Where the items they were given to cre-ate a calculation problem with were from the same category, the dupes would invariably choose an addition exercise; where they were thematically and not literally linked, they'd choose subtraction. The conclusion here is that the information you are processing in some way affects the way in which you might be programmed to process it; that we have differing cogni-tive leanings according to the differing content(s) we are dealing with.

FURTHER ARGUMENTS FOR DOMAIN-SPECIFIC COGNITION: EMBEDDED COGNITION

This is the argument that cognition is part of our very core, and that any attempt at an understanding of things is inextricably linked to our nature as physical beings. Cognition is therefore embedded in our very (physical) being. Imagine, if you will, that you are attempting to visit a great aunt in some strange and alien part of south-west Wales, and are completely and utterly lost. You ask a gurning local with white whiskers and a frayed bobble hat for directions and, as he explains to you the various turns and tributaries you must go down to reach the goal of auntie's house, he uses his right hand to almost mime the map in the air: turning his palm to face you for a right turn, away from you for a left turn. After he has done this, you repeat back to him what he has told you, doing the same actions in an attempt to internalise the turns you must take.

Your plenary here is miming the actions he has given you by engaging the sensory motor areas of the brain. These brain areas are often employed when seeking the solution to a problem and, interestingly, they are often employed in solving more abstract, less spatial issues than merely finding the directions to auntie's house.

Chris, the un-surnamed blogger behind 'Mixing Memory' comes up with a beauteous phrase to explain embodied cognition: it is a result of the 'tight coupling between an embodied organism and its environment'.[23] Embedded cognition, therefore, argues that cognition is inevitably tied to the environment and, consequently, you won't work things out in the same way in the science lab as you will in the language lab.

---

23 Available at http://mixingmemory.blogspot.co.uk/2004/12/reasoning-domain-general-vs-domain.html (accessed 22 May 2013).

ARGUMENTS FOR DOMAIN-SPECIFIC COGNITION: SITUATED COGNITION

There are four tenets of situated cognition, each of which is debatable.

1   **Action is grounded in the concrete situation in which it occurs**

This is the argument that darts players might be good at calculations when they are beered up on the oche, but will struggle, when eventually sober, while down the shops working out whether they can afford another four pack of McEwan's train beer. It is backed up by a study of Brazilian street children who could perform complex calculations on the streets, but were all at sea in a classroom. It is arguably nonsense. Learning probably does have an intimate relationship with the context in which something is learnt, but any suggestion that humans can't apply learning from one area to another seems suspect. I learned to write in Mr Latham's English class in a south-east London comp over thirty years ago. I don't go there any more. I am vastly too old, and the school doesn't actually exist any longer. But I do still employ the lessons Mr Latham taught me when the occasion is appropriate.

2   **Knowledge does not transfer between tasks**

On a pretty base level, this is contestable. To make a cup of tea you've got to put the kettle on. To make a Pot Noodle, what do you do first? You reach for the kettle, of course. However, as David Didau has pointed out to me, this is merely 'near transfer': the context of the original learning is extremely similar to the new learning here. Daisy Christodolou, author of *Seven Myths about Education*, contends that knowledge does not transfer between tasks where the intellectual distance between the tasks is substantial, 'Skills are tied to domain knowledge,' says Daisy. 'If you can analyse a poem, it doesn't mean you can analyse a quadratic equation, even though we apply the word "analysis" to each activity.'[24] You could argue here that 'analysis' is merely a synonym for entirely different functions, but my point here is not to debunk, merely to establish that what some might have you believe as fact is not entirely established as such. The question is whether 'far transfer' exists in any positive way? It is easy to see how maths would help you in statistics, more debatable whether the skills learnt in drama might help in a physics lesson. The transferability of knowledge/skills (which are broadly the same thing) is dependent on the proximity of the original learning to the new situation; whilst it is probable that Steven Spielberg would be a lousy coach for a baseball team, it is not certain, and the likelihood is that he would be a better coach than someone who had never before brought in a major project.

3 Training by abstraction is of little use

You could argue that this underestimates our intellectual abilities.

The late Harry S. Broudy, a Professor of Education from the United States, wrote convincingly about how the ability to transfer knowledge between tasks is related to the 'abstraction potential' of any one person: 'Some generalisation is required to apply ... skills to situations that were not practiced under the eye of a teacher. How to solve algebraic equations and how to decide which equations to use in a particular problem differ in their demands on the abstraction potential of the individual.'[25]

---

24 http://thewingtoheaven.wordpress.com/2013/06/15/
myth-five-we-should-teach-transferable-skills/

25 Harry S. Broudy, 'The Role of Imagery in Learning', Occasional Paper 1 (Los Angeles, CA: Getty Center for Education in the Arts, 1987), 9.

4   **Instruction must be done in complex social environments**

Again, nonsense. You can learn something on your own. You can learn by being told something. Here's proof. In 1959 Nottingham Forest beat Luton Town 2-1 in the FA Cup Final. Forest's first goal was scored by Roy Dwight, who then promptly broke his leg. He was Elton John's cousin. You now know that Elton John's cousin broke his leg whilst playing in the FA Cup Final for Notts Forest. You didn't learn it in a social environment and it wasn't a particular challenge learning it.

FURTHER ARGUMENTS FOR DOMAIN-SPECIFIC COGNITION: EVOLUTION AND MODULARITY

This feels as if it bears more weight than the others, and here we are firmly in the realms of the really, actually genuinely, quite interesting. There is an argument that cognition is modular – separated into distinct units – and that some knowledge is innate, genetic even. This is evidenced by, among other things, the fact that babies and small animals avoid steep vertical drops (if they can help it). You can't learn this by trial and error; for one error in this realm and all your trials would be over forever. They do this even if they've had no experience of falling before. Exploiting this, Australian naturalists have attempted an aversion therapy designed to stop the cat-sized marsupial, the quoll, from dying out from eating horrid, poisonous cane toads by feeding the quolls sausages featuring a combination of cane toad meat and brussel sprouts. They've found that the aversion that this develops in the quolls is passed down and that new generations of baby marsupials are born avoiding cane toads as they are inextricably associated, for them, with the foul taste of the sprout. Modular cognition in action! Cognition is an innate, pre-programmed module that has evolved and is specific to the area of cognition.

ARGUMENTS FOR COGNITION BEING DOMAIN GENERAL

This is best explained by someone else:

Another way to explain domain-specific effects in the literature is to refer to the distinction between active processing and automaticity. When people are learning how to perform a particular task, or to solve a particular type of problem, they tend to use domain-general processes. However, as they repeatedly encounter the same type of task, it becomes economical to store successful solutions as a whole. After these solutions are stored, people no longer need to use domain-general processes to solve those problems. Instead, they can simply retrieve the previously stored solution.

Thus, we're back where we started. There are cases that seem to entail domain-specific processing, but there may be domain-general explanations of those cases. Furthermore, domain-specific processes may actually be learned by using domain-general processes and storing specific solutions derived with them. Certainly there are some domain-specific modules in the brain ... However, because there is no conclusive evidence for a general view of cognition from either perspective, and since both tend to be able to explain the bulk of the data available, we're just going to have to wait for anything like a definitive answer.[26]

---

26 Available at http://mixingmemory.blogspot.co.uk/2004/12/reasoning-domain-general-vs-domain.html/ (accessed 22 May 2013).

So it seems, whilst there is no definitive solution, that in the initial stages of learning we are probably domain general; but, in repeating the same or similar task, we become domain specific as we attempt to achieve automaticity. When we are in the early stages of learning to drive we will attempt to apply whatever general principles related to memorising that we are in possession of; then, as we move towards automaticity in our use of the gear stick, the indicator, the clutch, our cognition becomes modular and specific to that particular action. It can be argued that the two positions are not actually mutually exclusive. We will apply domain-general processes at an early stage of learning and will then develop them into the specific.

What we can come to, though, is an understanding that many of the assertions about this are not entirely trustworthy. The idea that cognition is domain specific is not accepted fact, but is, moreover, part of an ongoing and completely unresolved dialogue amongst people with many letters after their names. One might be led to the conclusion that there is no undisputed proof that work on metacognition in one class *necessarily fails* to transfer to the next class, and that whole-school learning-to-learn programmes are, much against my own personal and very rabid prejudices, potentially of value to our students across subjects.

PART 2
ANALOGUE PLENARIES

And here we get to the probable reason that you bought the book. A series of off-the-shelf strategies you can apply in lessons. But beware, there are two sections. This first section is a series of ideas unreferenced to the research on metacognition, and are referred to as 'Analogue Plenaries', in that they are, in terms of their relationship to metacognitive plenaries, vinyl as opposed to CD. These are followed by an overlong disquisition on metacognition (Part 3), and following this, a set of activities (Part 4) that are a little more in tune with the research, and are more about developing students' powers of metacognition than they are about sticking the information from the lesson in their heads. These we will call 'Digital Plenaries', despite the fact that they have little connection with new technologies, but because they are the 2.0 of the plenary.

1. DON'T SHARE THE OBJECTIVES UNTIL THE END

While acknowledging my comments in Part 1 – that sharing objectives is actually a good idea – there is another way of looking at it, which is a fun idea and works if the class is sufficiently well routined. You don't share the objectives at the beginning, but at the end of the lesson you ask the students what they thought the objectives were. They sit in pairs or threes working out what they think you wanted them to learn in the lesson, and then discuss this in whatever brilliant grouping structure you deem appropriate and come to some kind of consensus.

This leads on to the very genius part of it: in the last three minutes you do the kind of 'reveal' much beloved of transformation television and slowly, with the seductive intent of Salome dancing the seven veils, reveal what the objectives really were. This might be used as the springboard for further discussion. But whatever the outcome of the reveal, we have here, finally, found a way of spelling out lesson objectives that transforms the experience for students from the 'This is the bit where the teacher plasters on a fake smile and acts as if they are preternaturally bored trawling through this sorry bag of balderdash one more time'.

2. START WITH A GAG

Tell a joke at the beginning of the lesson that requires subject-specific knowledge, and have as one of the objectives, 'By the end of this lesson you will be able to tell me why that joke is or is not funny'.

An example: one of the things that many English teachers are clearly not qualified to do is to analyse the decisions of a graphic designer as to what type, font size and so on they use. The fact that English teachers have no professional or technical understanding whatsoever of the thought processes of the graphic designer, does not stop this from being something that all students are examined on, and leads to every essay on presentation devices including the deathly, repetitive and amateur non-analysis: 'The designer does this to attract the readers' attention'. The fact that students use this sentence for every typographical device, no matter whether it is italics, capitalisation, bold, shadowing, colour choice, the lot, does not stop teachers from thinking that 'It attracts the readers' attention' is a useful trowel with which to miserably fail a very important exam.

What students do need to know about are the technical details and aesthetics of type. My lesson on this starts with the following, not particularly funny, gag.

I shot the serif.

Most students are dimly aware of a Bob Marley song by the same name, but have no idea what a serif is. Halfway through the lesson one of them twigs. But at the end, we ask them to analyse or unpack why the joke wasn't actually at all funny (preferably in writing).

The set-up to this is pretty easy: do a Google image search for 'typeface joke', 'quadratic equations joke' or 'design and technology joke'. There will be something there that requires the students to have understood a concept in order to analyse how the joke worked. Bung it on a PowerPoint at the beginning of the lesson, before you share the objectives, and you have an interesting plenary activity.

3. A PYRAMID OF PLENARY

This one is difficult to explain graphically on a portrait page. But here goes.

All make sense now? Good. We'll move on.

Oh, you need the headings ...

<u>One question you are left with</u>

<u>Two concepts you understand that you didn't know before</u>

<u>Three new pieces of vocabulary you now know and what they mean</u>[27]

The kids ask the question from the top of the pyramid. And you answer. Or better still, supervise while they work in groups answering each others' questions. You merely listen in and clarify if the answer is not available to them without your help. Alternatively, a suggestion that head teacher Simon Warburton made at the first ever London Teach Meet, in December 2012, can be used to enliven this one a little. He calls the questions 'exit tickets': you

---

27   This is best done as a poorly photocopied sheet in landscape rather than portrait.

must have one in order to leave the room at the end of the lesson, and that exit ticket becomes your homework. Simon, acknowledging that twenty-first century technology exists, and that the interweb has been invented, asks students to look up the answer themselves (perhaps even to come into the next lesson with it written up). Which is nice if they've got the interweb.

Some families can't afford it.

4. SHOW ME THE MONEY

There's a nice question that you can use here that would be beloved of various, erm, stakeholders, in British education, which is: 'How could you make money out of this information?'

The answers you get are interesting. It is a question that plausibly might ignite the dormant entrepreneurial spirit within the till now entirely innocent seven-year-old. But, most importantly, you start using the information in the lesson with a degree of excitement and effort, and forget that you are doing the plenary, the intention of which is to stick something boring in their heads.

5. PICK ON TWO STUDENTS

You might think that you have to tell the poor guinea pigs who they are at the beginning of the lesson. But think about it: if you don't, and you just pick the names out of a hat at the end of the lesson, then everyone's got to be on their toes all lesson. It could be you!

Instruct the class that at the end of the lesson you will be picking two people whom you are going to challenge on the learning in the lesson. And when you get to the point when you are performing the plenary, you punt in a series of quite focused questions at the two students you have selected. You are allowed to let other students make contributions, but once it has been thrown out to the floor you have to focus the new questioning towards the two selected students.

6. EXTENDED ABSTRACTION

This paragraph was written before reading anything in any depth about SOLO (Structure of Observed Learning Outcome) taxonomy, which, it appears from leafing through the interweb, it is de rigueur for teaching spods to have an opinion on. Thus far I've only skimmed over the five stages, and the final stage, *extended abstract*, on first glance speaks mightily as being two words that, once nestled together, create something that reaches far beyond their individual meanings. Extended: going on a bit. Abstract: riffing off on a tangent.

Of course, having now read up on SOLO in the gap between the end of the last paragraph and the beginning of this one, I now know that the extended abstract stage of SOLO is the stage of learning where one is able to make links between the learning and other areas; it is the stage where the majority of teachers might be inclined to go cross-curricular (so to speak). But let's go off on an extended abstraction about the plenary here. Initially it seems a mighty fine idea to ask students the question, 'How does this learning relate to science? To maths? To reading?' Until you actually try to do it yourself and find it doesn't, and that the question is just as likely to make students feel stupid because it's a crap question and there's no reasonable answer to it.

Here's a piece of knowledge that some struggle to attain: the man in the sky who watches everything you do, and who is not only in the sky but is in your toaster too; who knows when you are sleeping, knows when you're awake; who created the laws of physics, but decides not to be in any way bound by them; whom no one has *ever* seen, and who is the embodiment of love; but who will, somewhat paradoxically, condemn you to being poked with a sharp fork for all eternity if you, quite reasonably, point out that if no one has ever seen something, then it is fairly certain that that thing does not exist … Like football,[28] the premature sexualisation of working class females and *The Sun* newspaper, is just a load of cobblers to keep us all stupid enough to not spend any time questioning the methods by which the rich people stay rich and we stay poor.

Relate this new information to reading. It transports the Bible into the fiction section of the school library. But does it help you decode? You cannot relate this new learning to the mechanics of reading without that relationship being so forced as to be either utterly banal or completely surreal. Relate it to geography then. How, aside from us now knowing that God didn't put the rocks there with his massive invisible hand, does it throw any light on skree slopes? Quite simply, it doesn't. Relate it to 2 x 2 = 4. Aside from the scream, 'If God doesn't exist, then even the most simple mathematical equation is no longer trustworthy/even more trustworthy', this collision bears no light.

Perhaps this is a result of a faultily chosen, aberrant example. So, let's try another one: oxbow lakes are built by the sediment when a river meanders. Relate this to the study of literature, *Macbeth* for instance. Actually, don't bother. It's a complete waste of time, and would be for your pupils if you asked them to do the same. The version of the extended abstract under-standing we would most readily reach for – the cross-curricular tango, if you like – will actually result in a banal and pointless exercise for your students. So, next time you are tempted to conduct a plenary that asks students to identify three ways in which the lesson might be applied in other subjects, first check you can do it profitably yourself. You'll probably find you can't, or that you have to specify the subjects for it to work.

---

28 It is a little known, though utterly true, fact that football was actually invented by the Conservative Party in the late nineteenth century to ensure that working class males would never use their considerable energies to question the structures which kept them poor and stupid. 'Screw politics, Lamps has just broken the Chelsea all-time scorers' record.'

There's another possible approach that simply uses the two words, extended abstract, as a springboard, and jumps several stages of the SOLO taxonomy, directly into students creating art with the learning. If we take the Wikipedia definition of the extended abstract stage in which, 'The previous integrated whole may be conceptualised at a higher level of abstraction and generalised to a new topic or area',[29] and ditch the requisite that the learning has either been integrated or is in any way whole, we can still generalise it to a new topic or area as an attempt at making it integrated. We can still make something pretty with it; we can riff with it, we can do something interesting with the information.

We could use it as a stimulus with which to write: to produce an anecdote or an apology; to reflect on how it potentially amends our autobiography; we can review it; make a complaint about it; describe it; write an editorial about it; write an essay – a eulogy for our former ignorance; explain it; transform it into a fable, or fairy tales, or fantasy. We could transcribe an interview about it; construct a joke that is somehow related to it; ascribe it legendary status and write a story about it. We could write a letter to the learning; list all the things we will get out of it; construct a dramatic monologue; a news script. We might parody it; use it as the basis of a persuasive letter or speech; construct a short play featuring the learning as a character; write a poem about it (a villanelle, perhaps). We could retell it through another prism: review it in a broadsheet; transform it into science fiction; write a thank-you note or a tongue twister. Anything, in short. Anything at all that causes us to do *something* with the learning that not only makes us use it again – apply it, if you will – but also improves our skills at writing through giving us 'interesting' stimuli to write about.

But if we are to move into the realm of abstraction, then writing, perhaps, feels too concrete and leads us to wonder if an extended piece of abstract

---

29 Available at http://en.wikipedia.org/wiki/Structure_of_Observed_Learning_Outcome (accessed 22 May 2013).

work based on the learning were to really hit the brief, then we'd reach in the direction of the visual arts: doodle, sketch, cartoon, comic strip, paint the learning. We'd maybe lurch towards the dramatic: constructing a brief improvisation related to the learning (symbolic or realist), or we'd get out our 'jazz hands' and compose intriguing verses or repetitive choruses, replete with the hook lines that so resolutely avoided me when I was a musician.

The problem with the extended notion of this idea is that in a ten-minute plenary you are unlikely to have time to complete a chiaroscuro pencil drawing related to the learning in the style of da Vinci, as they usually take a little longer than ten minutes. Here you use what is called your professional judgement, altering the time frames of the lesson to accommodate a longer plenary, reserving this kind of activity to an end-of-week super plenary that takes all lesson, or resigning yourself to the fact that the task will be started but not necessarily finished.

7. WHAT IS THE EXACT OPPOSITE OF WHAT YOU HAVE LEARNT IN THIS LESSON? (WHAT IS A TANGENT TO IT?)

It's an apparently simple enough question, but it can take a bit of a wild cognitive leap till we get interesting answers. Of course, the opposite of learning that something does something is learning that it doesn't; and so, we have to take a creative line with the questioning here. What is the opposite of 'heat makes things expand'? will generally be greeted with the response, 'Heat doesn't make things expand'. But once you ban that response, request that your students don't immediately grasp towards the obvious, as it is no way to live a life, then ask kids to find a *real* opposite that exists outside of the realms of the easy negative you will get, 'Cold makes things retract'. Which is nice. But where it gets really interesting is when we ask, what is a tangent to the knowledge? Here we are in exciting territory. A ten-year-old with whom I live came up with 'Cold makes things solidify'. A worthy concept in itself, but a lovely little riff off the initial piece of knowledge, which we revisit – again, straightaway – in order to ensure that it is an established piece of knowledge lodged in the student's brain.

Alternatively, we could ensure that we ask a question when we are plenarising that is not, in any way, binary. Try finding the opposite of the following: there are two versions of the apostrophe: contractive and possessive. Does this have an opposite? Ask a ten-year-old and you get the following response: 'No. But if it did have an opposite it would be speech marks.'

'Why?'

'One way is that it's upside down – it's therefore opposite in looks. The other way is you show speech with speech marks and with apostrophes you show possession.'

'What would a tangent to it be?'

'There's one version of the full stop [only there isn't: abbreviations].'

Does it matter if we can't find a properly cohesive answer? We are still involved in thinking deeply about the main learning point.

It helps students understand what you are going on about if you present the question to them with a little graphical aid.

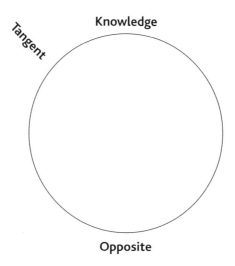

8. THE FROZEN PICTURE

I've written about this before in my first book, *Could Do Better*,[30] and in my fifth book, *Dancing about Architecture*.[31] So apologies if you are one of the three people who purchased either of those books and have this one too. Briefly, a frozen picture is a fairly stock drama technique in which groups of students freeze in various positions to create a pictorial dramatic snapshot of a moment in time. They come in two varieties: naturalistic and symbolic. The naturalistic is easy to understand, relatively easy to apply and perhaps not as interesting. To save me from scribing anything new I am now going briefly enjoy the cardinal luxury of ultimate self-indulgence: quoting one's self:

> The kids act as if they were unconsciously caught by a camera, the action frozen. Being naturalistic, it captures moments from some dramatic approximation of reality: the moment Mandela was released, the moment they went over the trenches in the First World War, a mother lamenting a dying child in the Ethiopian famine. Anything that would make an interesting tableau that illuminates the curriculum.[32]

A good naturalistic (or indeed symbolic) frozen picture will have the following characteristics: kids will be stood stock still, having previously located/

---

30 Which isn't really much good at all. Don't bother.
31 Which is, or so I thought, a paradigm-shifting work of the rarest genius; and is certainly better than some of the brain-dead reviewers on Amazon suggest: 'It was a bit whacky'. I ask you ...? Do bother.
32 Phil Beadle, *Dancing about Architecture: A Little Book of Creativity* (Carmarthen: Crown House, 2011), 33.

identified their centre of gravity, they will have located a focus point, at which they are grimly staring; and it will feature a variety of spatial levels.

The symbolic frozen picture is more interesting and is probably more appropriate for the plenary than the naturalistic version. In it, students don't necessarily play the parts of humans: they can play objects, concepts, abstractions. 'They can instead be taken, in freeze-frame, to represent ideas, concepts, themes or even a specific analysis of a text or historical event.'[33] Or they can get into a formation that somehow encapsulates the learning in the lesson. It is the open-ended nature of this activity that leads to it having such interesting results. Also, in bringing the concrete to the abstract, the students are using high-order thinking skills that partially, at least, reflect the last stage of SOLO.

If you are drama averse (and many are) you can achieve the same effects by getting the kids to draw the frozen picture they might have done if their teacher wasn't quite such a wimp.

The beauty of either of these activities is that, even with preparation time, they hit the ten-minute time frame of the plenary bang on the nose. Show the frozen pictures and get students to evaluate how well they sum up the learning and you have a real student-pleaser on your hands.

---

33   Beadle, *Dancing about Architecture,* 37.

9. MIME THE LEARNING

THIS PAGE HAS NOT BEEN LEFT ACCIDENTALLY BLANK.[34]

---

34 Reread the section in Part 1 on embedded cognition on page 30. This is not nearly as stupid an idea as it seems.

10. KEY WORD STORYTELLING

This is another idea I have written about under another cover. So apologies if you are one of the literally tens of people who have a copy of *How to Teach*.[35] But it's such a doozie it bears repeating. It's also the object of a gratifying ego trip since I've been doing observations in a couple of schools to write reports on how the teaching and learning culture of the school could be improved and witnessed this being used as a plenary a few times. It has spread for a reason: it works and it's fun.

Loosely, you collect the key words for a lesson, or preferably a string of lessons, put them into four columns and ask kids in groups of four to create a story one sentence at a time in which the key words are used. The story must start with 'Once upon a time ...', and it often helps if the lead character is a mouse.

Year 9: Volcanoes – Key Words

Student 1	Student 2	Student 3	Student 4
Active Crater Lava	Ash Crust Magma	Dust Dormant	Core Extinct

---

35 Phil Beadle, *How to Teach* (Carmarthen: Crown House, 2010).

Once upon a time there lived a not very active mouse by the name of Monty. Monty smoked far too many cigarettes and, consequently, his bri-nylon tracksuit was all too often covered with ash. Though he tried to keep himself looking relatively spruce by wiping down his trackie with a dust cloth, he looked a right state. When Monty's mummy saw him, his awful appearance rocked her to her core. He had eyes like sunken ships and craters where his cheeks should be. A permanent pie-crust clogged up his tear ducts. He was the quintessence of dormant.

Monty's mummy wondered whether he might soon be extinct. But he just spent all his days staring vacantly into the lava lamp as it bubbled. Spots erupting like magma …

You get the point. The students get to reuse the key language from the lessons in an amusing way. It's far better when they do it in groups, as the wild card of having it constructed by different people makes it go off in lovely tangential directions; when an adult writes one on their own it just becomes poorly disguised, and arguably tragic, autobiography.

11. KEY WORD DEFINITION MATCHING

This is an activity many teachers will be inclined to use as a starter, but which is actually better as a plenary, as by the end of the lesson they actually have the information they need to do it and don't have to rely on inference and deduction, which can be problematic before cognition has really engaged. Create a table, like the one below, in which the correct definitions are in the wrong places. Students have to draw lines from the key word to the correct definition. If you like you can give them scissors to play with too.

Key word	Definition
Geneva	A highly legible Roman type which provided the letters for the American Declaration of Independence
Garamond	A traditional and 'chilly' front designed for *The Times* newspaper in 1931. It is ubiquitous and a bit boring. Deliberately not 'different' or 'jolly'
Comic Sans	Very similar font to Times New Roman, but with wider serifs
Times New Roman	Clean Swiss letters reflecting corporate modernism
Georgia	Looks as if it was written by an eleven-year-old: smooth and rounded letters, nothing unexpected, the sort of shapes that would appear in alphabet soup. You can imagine it with each letter in a different colour

A further variant of this, which leads to kids bumping into each other, and might have an observer writing the dread words 'health and safety' on their observation sheet, is to give half the students a key word and the other half a definition and get them to wander aimlessly around the room, deliberately bumping into each other, attempting to find their other half.

(This takes a hell of a lot of prep in terms of cutting up, so it's better if you just give the kids the sheets with definitions and key terms on it and get them to cut them up.)

12. PELMANISM

You'll know the game from your childhood (hopefully, you're not currently spending your evenings playing it, as that is a bad sign) but you'll probably know it by the name of 'Concentration' or 'Pairs'.

Like in the card game for lonely people, students lay out the key terms and the definitions face down on their desk. The first student flips two cards over and if they match, shouts 'Hurrah', puts them to the side and has another go. Mostly, though, they won't match and after kid one has expressed disappointment, kid two dives in and turns first one card, then two, over. Of course, if on the first turn he has found the definition to the key word that kid one turned over, he cracks into a smug smile and turns that over, claiming a pair and getting another go. The winner is the one with the most pairs.

So far so boring, but there's more. It comes in a series of fascinating varieties:

- **One Flip:** Where you don't get an extra go if you get a pair.

- **Fancy:** You lay the upside-down pieces of paper in a strict rectangular grid.

- **Spaghetti:** You lay them randomly on the floor. On the floor, I said. Did you hear me? On the floor! Randomly. I'm not kidding ya!

13. DO IT YOURSELF WILL YA?

All the students in the class have to write down a question related to the . learning on a single piece of paper. These are then screwed up and delivered to teacher who, handily, has an empty shoe box in which to keep them.

You then put the kids into pairs, fours or, preferably, threes and ask the questions. They have to come to an answer within thirty seconds, before you fire off another question.

It doesn't matter that their answers to the questions are wrong. As they are not shared, no one gets to know.

14. QUIZZES

One of the hoary old clichés of the plenary is the 'Who Wants to be a Millionaire?' quiz-type thing. It's a quiz on the learning. Be excited. Yowsah, it's a quiz. It's Blockbusters. Quizzes are fun. Aren't they? It's a worthy quiz. It's not necessarily a completely useless idea. It's a quiz on the learning. It's what everyone does. It's a quiz on the learning.

It's not up to much really, is it? It's a quiz on the learning. It's a bit shit. It's a quiz on the learning.

A more cognitive way of doing things is asking students to design questions about the learning they think would be relevant if they were question-setters on some banal piece of daytime pass-the-time-as-we-are-waiting-for-our-please-come-soon-death programming on the idiot box. That is enough, of course. But if you want to over-egg the mixed metaphor, then you can get kids into pairs, and they ask each other the questions.

A further level of this is to get them to differentiate — see how much they like it! — so that they, themselves, produce a series of quiz (Yes! A quiz!) questions under the headings easy/hard/very hard; vegetable/routine/spod; special needs/mainstream/G&T axis.

15. TABOO™

This is a lovely activity much beloved of geography advanced skills teachers. If you've not come across it, you give students a set of the key language from the lesson on paper or card (screwed up or cut nicely). These can be presented in either a bag or a box and then the students work in pairs or threes. One child chooses a word and has to describe the concept embodied by the word without using the word itself. The other member(s) of the pair or three has to guess what the word is. Good for developing oracy; double good for developing presenting skills if you get one child to attempt this activity in front of the rest of the class. It works best with a time limit.

16. DRINKING GAMES

My brother and I have a game that we play once a year, every single year, without fail, on Christmas Day. We sit in my front room with a bottle of scotch each. We drink our individual bottles of scotch whilst gossiping about stuff. Once we have fully downed our bottles, one of us has to leave the room and knock on the door; the other has to guess who it is. It is not at all easy!

I do not suggest you attempt this game in a classroom! (Firstly, my brother is busy mending pumps and is rarely, if ever, available on a weekday; secondly, though you'll find children are more malleable behaviourally after the first scotch has taken the edge off their paranoia, they really can't hold their drink, and go completely stupid after about ten minutes.)

Where drinking games can be used in a classroom is in terms of making the intrinsically dull rather more interesting. There is a good game (which I can only barely recall as I last played it twenty years ago in Andalucía, and was hammered at the time). Person 1 has to say the name of an unarguably crap celebrity: Harold Shipman,[36] for instance; Person 2 must then say the name of another famous person, whose name begins with the last letter of the name of Person 1's celeb. In this instance, Norman Collier[37] would do the trick. Person 3 then has to find the name of a famous person whose name begins with an 'r' (e.g. Robert Morley). You get the drift. If you are unable to locate a crap celebrity within the space of a minute you have to do some drinking.

---

36 Northern doctor who enjoyed murdering people.
37 Dead northern comedian famous for: 1) impersonating a chicken and 2) pretending he had a faulty microphone.

Try a version of this without the drink. Get one child to say what they have learnt in the lesson, then the next must start their sentence (in which they also must say what they have learnt) with a word that begins with the same letter the last sentence ended with.

17. SPOT THE DELIBERATE MISTAKE

Once upon a time there was a Scottish nobleman by the name of Macbeth. He was the son of Sinel, the much loved Thane of Cawdor,[38] and his best friend was a man called Banquo.[39] Whilst returning from a battle he had won (almost single handedly) travelling across the teeth[40] in the direction of Forres, Macbeth (and Banquo) bump into[41] three things that look like women, but who have moustaches.[42] They greet Macbeth and Banquo with three prophesies each:[43] telling Macbeth he will eventually be king, and that, though Banquo won't ever be king himself, his descendents will.

Macbeth is much taken with the idea of being king and writes to his wife about the predictions, who is also much taken with it and immediately starts planning to kill King Malcolm[44] who, by some strange coincidence, is staying at their castle that very evening. She calls for the spirits to make her into a

38 'Oo! Oo! I saw two mistakes. Sinel was the Thane of Glams and it is presumption to say that Cawdor was loved.'
39 'Oo! Oo! I saw a mistake. People always describe Banquo and Macbeth as being buddies but there is no evidence that they were anything more intimate than colleagues.'
40 'Oo! Oo! I saw a mistake. Heath.'
41 'Oo! Oo! I saw a mistake. Unless metaphorical.'
42 'Oo! Oo! I saw a mistake. Beards.'
43 'Oo! Oo! I saw a mistake. The first of the prophesies can't really be considered a prophesy as it has already happened. Macbeth's dad is already dead. It is crap sooth-saying to suggest that Macbeth will inherit his title. He has already inherited it. Also Banquo's first two: "Lesser than, greater than", "happier, less happy", aren't really prophesying anything at all. He's hardly more happy. He only lasts another fifteen minutes before he gets fifty gashes in his head and is killed.'
44 'Oo! Oo! I saw a mistake. King Duncan.'

man, even going so far as to suggest she wants her vagina plugged up so that she does not have a period and go silly.[45]

This is a really quite simple technique, but as you can see from the above you can have a lot of fun with it. The teacher writes a piece of text that is riddled with, erm, schoolboy errors and either shares this in written form or reads it out. The practical and logistical application of the technique is entirely up to you.

---

45   'Oo! Oo! I saw a mistake. That is some sexism on the part of the author.' (It isn't some sexism. She does say this.)

18. RE-ORDERING OR RE-SEQUENCING A TEXT

In the olden days this would have been a truly analogue task. You gave the children a text, which you had cut up and placed in an envelope; perhaps you'd have the cut pieces attached to each other with a paperclip. During the lesson the students would then have to put that text back together in its proper sequence. Nowadays, they have things called word processors and you do not have to waste all day Sunday cutting up things and putting them into envelopes. Cut and paste some information from a source into a Word document, then re-order it and print it out for your students.

Pleasingly, this makes the task actually vastly more cognitive than the analogue version of it. As, in truth, you do not even have to be able to read to perform the paper version, as the cut-up pieces of paper will ordinarily have patterns, indentations, etc. that will make it entirely possible to reconstruct the A4 piece of paper like you would do a jigsaw puzzle (in Braille).

See if you can re-sequence the following example into chronological order:

Miss the deadline three separate times
Note that the book on starters and plenaries doesn't do so badly
Be somewhat at a loss as to what to write your next book about
Make disappointed face as they offer you a contract
Spend six long, desolate months trying to make the dull undull
Resolve that next book will be on something you find interesting
Realise you've already written that you think starters are a total waste of time
Read really loads of boring research papers on metacognition
Look on Amazon
Suggest that you write a book on plenaries to your publisher

19. WHAT'S THE QUESTION?

The answer's 'Once on a Sunday with your mother'. What's the question? Keep it clean. The answer's 'Cock Robin'. What's the ...?

Beyond the remit of the blue pub pun this has some validity as a plenary activity. It also comes with the benefit of being very easy to prepare and potentially causes students to indulge in quite high order discursive activity in fluid Standard English. The ease of preparation is its chief selling point, though. Just set students into pairs or threes and use the key words from the lesson as the material. If we just take a Year 8 scheme of work from art as an example, we might set students the following conundrums:

1   The answer is 'manipulate'. What is the question?

2   The answer is 'mould'. What is the question?

3   The answer is 'observe'. What is the question?

4   The answer is 'overlay'. What is the question?

You can see here that it includes its own gifted and talented differentiation, in that those vibrating on a different string to others might choose to have fun with it. As such, it might be advisable to set three categories: lesson, literal and silly:

1   The answer is 'manipulate'. What is the question related to the lesson's learning?

2   The answer is 'manipulate'. What is the question, literally?

3   The answer is 'manipulate'. What could be a silly question to get this answer?

You don't need me to provide the answers to this. Have a go yourself.

20. DIAGRAMMATIC REPRESENTATION

A pleasingly free-form activity is to take the information from the lesson from textual representation to graphic. The most famous of these was not actually invented by Johnny Venn in the 1880s. You know what a Venn diagram is: overlapping circles to show whether something belongs in this set, that set, both sets or neither (in which case they live ostracised, outside the circle). They must contain an overlap, whereas the Venn diagram's close cousin, the Euler diagram doesn't. I won't waste your time any further. Here is a visual explanation.

Venn diagram about the relationship between cheese and dairy products

Euler diagram about 'All Things Bright and Beautiful'

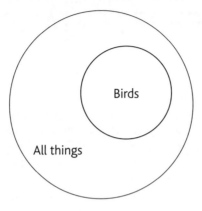

More complicated Euler diagram about 'All Things Bright and Beautiful'

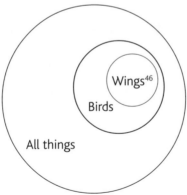

---

46 This is very, very funny. If you do not find it funny you are rubbish. It is ripped off from comedian Stewart Lee. God made 'all of them' you see: 'glowing colours', 'tiny wings', the lot.

CARROLL DIAGRAMS

Named after their inventor, Lewis (who is famous for something else), these show if something is in the set or isn't in the set. You can extend them out to be really complicated.

This one is simple:

Fish	Not fish
Haddock	Haribo
Ling	Denizens of Whitby
Cod	Shirley Conran
Salmon	Jamie Redknapp[47]
Dace	Tedium

So is this:

Things	Not things
Tyres	
Trousers	
Radiator keys	
Wisdom	

---

47 Who is not a fish. He just looks like one.

This is a little more complicated:[48]

	Gay	Not gay
Funny		Stewart Lee Simon Munnery Al Murray Vic and Bob
Not funny	Alan Carr 4 Poofs and a Piano Graham Norton Rhona Cameron Sue Perkins (comedienne) (!) Julian Clary David Walliams	Richard Herring David Walliams

---

48 This did not start off with the intention of being homophobic. But you find stuff out doing these diagrams.

This is a bit more complicated:

	Talentless	Moderately talented	Very talented	Virtuoso
White	Lily Allen Jim Morrison Robbie Williams Gary Barlow The other three	Lou Reed Mick Jagger Bono	John Lennon Eminem Kurt Cobain Elton John	
Black	Joss Stone	Bob Marley	Public Enemy	Jimi Hendrix Stevie Wonder B. B. King Al Green Marvin Gaye Miles Davis Herbie Hancock Ray Charles Aretha Franklin

ISHIKAWA DIAGRAMS

Otherwise known as fishbone diagrams, Ishikawa diagrams, which we've imported into education from the Kawasaki shipyards in Japan where they were first used, show cause and effect.

Current causes of unemployability

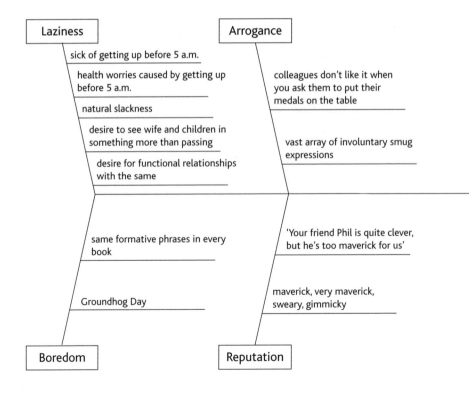

Insolence

inability to cope with hierarchical structures

inability to stop taking the mick

not good at singing the company song without inventing silly, satirical lyrics

occasional graffiti crimes
(often involving forlorn, wilting penises)

deliberately sitting slightly too close to colleagues to wind them up

always having more in common with the guy on the competency than anyone else

Result
no head teacher will touch me with a bargepole

can't handle ties

don't like shoes, don't like polishing shoes, rubbish at polishing shoes, never polishes shoes

aftershave too florid

bored of going to drycleaners

looking like I've been set on fire and put out with a spade

Presentation

MIND MAPS

Mind maps are hoary and, of course, take vastly too long to do with any degree of exactitude to be of any use for a ten-minute plenary activity. But here's an idea: what would be the outcome of each child in your class having a piece of A3 paper which they keep at the back of their exercise books; a mind map of the learning they have encountered in the whole scheme of work, which they add to for ten minutes at the end of every lesson; specifically, with the new learning that they have acquired in this particular lesson? The kids would have a ready visual reminder of everything relevant to them that they had learned in the whole half term (which, not entirely incidentally, looks great on the wall).

21. SPACED REPETITION

The idea for this came from an article in *The Guardian* Education pages by David Cox, who is (so it says here) a computational student of neuroscience. He cleverly points out that if you play music when you are revising you're probably giving your brain too many things to do. Cox informs us that memory is based on 'the brain's neuroplasticity, its ability to reorganise itself throughout your life by breaking and forming new connections between its billions of cells'.[49] These 'pathways between neurons' can be strengthened by repetition which 'consolidates the pattern'. But there is a scientific aspect to this that an interested practitioner might apply their imagination and passion to in order to obtain the best for their students. Cox speaks of a concept called 'spaced repetition':

> Science tells us the ideal time to revise what you've learned is just before you're about to forget it. And because memories get stronger the more you retrieve them, you should wait exponentially longer each time – after a few minutes, then a few hours, then a day, then a few days. This technique is known as spaced repetition.[50]

This also explains why you forget things so quickly after a week of cramming for an exam. Because the exponential curve of memory retrieval does not continue, the process reverses and within a few weeks you've forgotten everything you've learnt!

---

49 David Cox, 'How Your Brain Likes to be Treated at Revision Time'. Available at http://www.guardian.co.uk/education/mortarboard/2012/nov/06/how-your-brain-likes-to-revise (accessed 22 May 2013).
50 Cox, 'How Your Brain Likes to be Treated at Revision Time'.

Logistically, this is a nightmare of organisation. But it is merely a case of doing the maths: over the space of two weeks when starting a new scheme of work (or particularly if you are running revision sessions in which you want recall of the knowledge to really stick) your plenary schedule with spaced repetition might look something like this.

Day (Week)	
Monday (1)	Standard plenary recalling information from Monday 1
Tuesday (1)	Standard plenary recalling information from Tuesday 1 Recap on information from Monday 1
Wednesday (1)	Standard plenary recalling information from Wednesday 1 Recap on information from Tuesday 1
Thursday (1)	Standard plenary recalling information from Thursday 1 Recap on information from Wednesday 1 Further recap on information from Monday 1
Friday (1)	Standard plenary recalling information from Friday 1 Recap on information from Thursday 1 Further recap on information from Tuesday 1

Day (Week)	
Monday (2)	Standard plenary recalling information from Monday 2 Recap on information from Friday 1 Further recap on information from Wednesday 1
Tuesday (2)	Standard plenary recalling information from Tuesday 2 Recap on information from Monday 2 Further recap on information from Thursday 1
Wednesday (2)	Standard plenary recalling information from Wednesday 2 Recap on information from Tuesday 2 Further recap on information from Friday 1
Thursday (2)	Standard plenary recalling information from Thursday 2 Recap on information from Wednesday 2 Further recap on information from Monday 2 Additional recap on information from Monday 1
Friday (2)	Standard plenary recalling information from Friday 2 Recap on information from Thursday 2 Further recap on information from Tuesday 2 Additional recap on information from Tuesday 1

On first sight this looks like an administrative ordeal since, as time goes by, you accumulate more and more pieces of information that have to be plenarised, and clearly there will come a point at which it is too unwieldy to continue. However, the logic of this idea is solid, and if we really want our students to remember what we have studied in lessons, then in terms of results, this idea has substantial promise, particularly in the lead-up to exams.

22. THE PLENARY OF PLENARIES

This idea is based upon the work of Fiona Lawton, senior lecturer in mathematics education at the University of Cumbria. In 2002 and 2003 Fiona undertook a 'small-scale practitioner research' for her master's degree,[51] which is one of the more interesting looks at how the plenary works and the levels of understanding it inculcates. Her findings were that the control group who had not been subjected to 'serious' plenaries in their training referred to them only on the basis of the subject-related learning; whereas those groups of student teachers who had been subject to intervention in terms of their understanding of what constituted a plenary had consciousness of a range of potential areas in which the plenary might have an effect. Fiona maps out five different 'dimensions of learning' on which the focus on the plenary might have an impact in terms of teacher knowledge: social, emotional, mathematical (for which read subject knowledge), metacognitive and professional.

The *social dimension* is lessons learnt in terms of relationships with others: group communication, team work, others as stimulus. The *emotional dimension* is the relationship that the learner has with their own emotional state and how this impacts upon their learning: how they feel when stuck with a problem, how they cope with perceived failure. The *subject-specific dimension* is clearly what curricular information they have picked up from the

---

51 Fiona Lawton, 'Using the Plenary to Develop Reflective and Critical Thinking and to Enhance Metacognitive Awareness: Student Teachers' Perceptions and School-Based Experiences of the Daily Mathematics Lesson Plenary', *Proceedings of the British Society for Research into Learning Mathematics* 24(2): 63–67.

lesson (and specifically the plenary). The *metacognitive dimension* (which is evidently related to the emotional dimension) is a reflection on their own 'learning strategies'. The *professional dimension* is specific to the fact that this was a study of student teachers and how they accreted professional knowledge.

We can use Lawton's headings as a structure with which we might conduct a plenary that hits every aspect or dimension of learning that it might reasonably be expected to do.

And so the Plenary of Plenaries merely asks students questions under headings. In pairs or groups we throw in the questions:

1   Did we learn anything about our relationships with each other during the lesson?

2   Did we learn anything about our emotional state when we were learning?

3   What did we learn about the subject?

4   Did we learn anything about learning itself?

PART 3
METACOGNITION FOR BEGINNERS

I am absolutely convinced that there is, overall, far too little rather than enough or too much cognitive monitoring in this world.

John H. Flavell[52]

It's almost impossible not to look at the above quote without letting out the tiniest, lightly parched sliver of a satirical fart. But Flavell is one of the Godheads of metacognition and his thoughts on it, though dense, are worth trying to translate so that they can have some practical application in the classroom. And that is the point of this section of the book: to look at what the academics say about things and see if, over the space of a few barren pages, we can attempt to construct a partial bridge over the academic/practitioner divide.

The original intention of this book has now been fulfilled. A series of (not many) activities have been outlined, and they might plausibly be used in the last ten minutes of a lesson. But, in the words of crap 1970s comic Jimmy Cricket, 'There's more'. If the plenary is to be a properly metacognitive strategy, and this book is actually to be a serious attempt at engaging with ideas about metacognition, then it is going to have to do a little better than that.

---

52 John H. Flavell, 'Metacognition and Cognitive Monitoring: A New Area of Cognitive/Developmental Inquiry', *American Psychologist* 34(10) (1979): 906–911, at 907.

If this book is to be something that you can attempt to apply which has the intention of making a real difference to the abilities of your students to improve their learning, or if it is to somehow reframe teachers' ideas of what is possible, then it is going to have to engage with some research and give suggestions as to how you might consider applying that research in a classroom situation to help your students take command of their learning.

Firstly, let's have a look at why teachers might want to engage with ideas regarding metacognition. The Sutton Trust's Toolkit (which is, at least and at best, a penetrable look at the effect size and relative cost of varying teaching strategies) lists metacognitive and self-regulation strategies as the second most effective means of improving student outcomes.[53] In the section 'How Effective Is It?', the authors report: 'Meta-cognitive approaches have a consistently high or very high levels of impact with meta-analyses reporting effect sizes between 0.59 and 0.73. These are substantial gains equivalent to moving a class from 50th place in a league table of 100 schools to about 25th. Encouragingly there is also evidence it is particularly helpful for low achieving pupils. Impact summary: +8 months (effect size 0.67).'[54]

Now, you might want to question what a class would be doing in a league table of schools, but the findings are in keeping with what Hattie reports around metacognition. Strategies aimed at improving powers of metacognition work!

53   Steve Higgins, Maria Katsipataki, Dimitra Kokotsaki, Robbie Coleman, Lee Elliot Major and Rob Coe, *The Sutton Trust – Education Endowment Foundation Teaching and Learning Toolkit* (London: Education Endowment Foundation, 2013).
54   Higgins et al., *Education Endowment Foundation Teaching and Learning Toolkit*, 19.

What, then, are these strategies? The Sutton Trust describes metacognition and self-regulation as:

> Teaching pupils strategies to plan, monitor and evaluate their own learning. It is usually more effective in small groups so learners can support each other and make their thinking explicit through discussion. Self-regulation refers to managing one's own motivation towards learning as well as the more cognitive aspects of thinking and reasoning.[55]

The authors go on to assess the strength of the evidence as being very strong and the potential cost implications for schools as being low.

Given the alleged panacea-like qualities of metacognition it seems a professional dictate that we investigate its potential relevance with some rigour or passion. The potentially off-putting aspect, and perhaps an explanation of why this is the first intentionally populist text that rubs up against the subject with a desire for any real friction, is that the moment teachers see five-syllable phrases featuring a Greek or Latin prefix they start imagining that it is the realm of science/experimental psychology and that it will be very difficult indeed. It is, quite. But relax. I'll translate.

In order to do so we'll first take a brief look at goal orientation theory and its relationship with our students' success, then examine the impact that the goals our students identify to themselves (or have as unconscious drivers) have on their powers of metacognition.

---

55 Higgins et al., *Education Endowment Foundation Teaching and Learning Toolkit*, 19. The second sentence here is completely un-evidenced.

GOAL ORIENTATION THEORY

Goal orientation theory looks at the motivation one might have in completing a (complex) learning task and broadly separates it into the desire for mastery and into two discrete performance-related motivations. Mastery is where 'the student's sense of satisfaction with the work is not influenced by external performance indicators such as grades'[56] and is 'associated with deeper engagement with the task and greater perseverance in the face of setbacks'. It is when you are climbing up a mountain so that you can see the world, not so the world can see you. And it is distinct from performance goals, in which the student judges themself in relation to the relative performance of others, and in which the desire for a better grade than our friends or rivals is a key motivating factor. A desire for mastery is intrinsic, while a desire to achieve a performance that is successful relative to others is clearly motivated by some arguably wafery extrinsic reward; and, in terms of learning, having mastery as a goal is a vastly more successful strategy than the performance motivations.

Kaplan and Maehr, whose paper 'The Contributions and Prospects of Goal Orientation Theory' examines the various evolutions and controversies in this field of study, define the distinction that separates 'mastery' and 'performance' as being the distinction between *developing* competence and *demonstrating* competence.[57] It makes sense that one is more successful than the other in that to seek to demonstrate competence you do not necessarily have to have attained it; a thin veneer might be enough to achieve your performance goal.

---

56   Carol Ames, 'Classrooms: Goals, Structures and Student Motivation', *Journal of Educational Psychology* 84(3): 261–271, at 263.
57   Avi Kaplan and Martin L. Maehr, 'The Contributions and Prospects of Goal Orientation Theory', *Educational Psychology Review* 19(2) (2007): 141–184.

A goal of developing competence rather than demonstrating (or even displaying) it is said to be associated with 'positive outcomes such as self efficacy, persistence, preference for challenge, self regulated learning, and positive affect and well-being'.[58]

Performance orientation is conversely and, of course, darn well guaranteed to turn you into a poly-drug-addicted, sexually profligate crazy by the time you are eighteen, and is reported to make you nervier, more anxious, less likely to be satisfied and more likely to cheat or to learn things on a superficial level. It also comes with an earth-shattering slap in the face should you fail, from which your shattered self-esteem may never fully recover.

For Kaplan and Maehr, the ego-driven desire to be seen or judged against others comes in two forms: 'performance approach' and 'performance avoidance'. The former is about wanting to be seen positively when judged against others; the latter about not wanting to be seen negatively. Both might be argued to be doomed attempts to somehow hold on to our self-concept as being clever, or funny, or sexy, or whatever other quality we might deem enviable.

Of course, this stuff comes with all kinds of caveats and glitches and irregularities with the research. Having mastery as your goal in a task tends to help you score highly on more complex, open-ended tasks, but does nothing for multi-choice comprehension questions, or for answering questions for which there is a correct one word answer.[59] Kaplan and Maehr cite a meta-analysis

---

58   Kaplan and Maehr, 'The Contributions and Prospects of Goal Orientation Theory', 142–143.
59   Kaplan and Maehr, 'The Contributions and Prospects of Goal Orientation Theory', 143.

by Christopher Utman which has revealed some broad brush strokes about goal orientation that may be taken as bearing some fairly useful truths:[60]

- Overall, mastery goals have a moderate effect on performance when compared to performance goals.

- The effect of mastery goals becomes large when the task is complex.

- The effect is non-existent when the task is simple.

- Older children and young adults benefit from mastery goals more than young children.

- Mastery goals have a greater effect when in a situation with others than when alone.

Whether this 'situation with others' is when we are situated in a class-room, when we are in competition or when we are working in groups is not explained, but it is unequivocal that older children, particularly when working on a more complex task, benefit from having the various goal orientations outlined to them, and for the correct goal orientation to be identified and for them to assimilate this as the bedrock of their work on metacognition.

---

60 Christopher H. Utman, 'Performance Effects of Motivational States: A Meta-Analysis', *Personality and Social Psychology Review* 1 (1997): 170–182, cited in Kaplan and Maehr, 'The Contributions and Prospects of Goal Orientation Theory', 144.

GOAL ORIENTATION AND METACOGNITION

Jeff Huang, whose 'Building an E-Portfolio Learning Model: Goal Orientation and Metacognitive Strategies' is an interesting read, if your idea of an interesting read is something that is deeply and unambiguously uninteresting, looks at these three versions of motivation and further hypothesises about their effect(s) on students.[61] Huang and colleagues link the effect of the three varieties of motivation to the incidence or effectiveness of students' metacognitive/self-regulation strategies, observing that a desire for mastery has an unambiguously positive effect, whilst the desire to not look daft (performance avoidance) has an unambiguously negative effect on self-regulation, and, most interestingly, the desire to show off has a slightly more ambiguous effect that only borders on being negative.

'Alright, and so what? You've read a research document. Get to the point.'

The point is that if we want to develop students' metacognitive knowledge and ability to self-regulate, we must teach them first what the correct approach to motivation is. They must set about tasks with the desire to master the task, rather than giving a fig about external reward or what anyone thinks of them.

(On a related tangent, the reason I have taken a subject that it is near impossible to become excited about for my seventh book on teaching and learning is not for the sales. (Hell no – the marketing is likely to read, 'If you only buy one book on metacognitive strategies to apply in the last ten minutes of a lesson this year, make it this one!') Nor is it for the glowing reviews in the many broadsheet newspapers that take an interest in the plenary as a concept. Nor even for the unadulterated, unabashed glamour of it all. The

---

61 Jeff J. S. Huang, Stephen J. H. Yang, Poky Y. F. Chiang and Luis S. Y. Tzeng, 'Building an E-Portfolio Learning Model: Goal Orientation and Metacognitive Strategies', *Knowledge Management & E-Learning: An International Journal* 4(1) (2012): 16–36.

reason I have taken a subject that it is near impossible to become excited about for my seventh book on teaching and learning is because I wanted to see if I could take on a challenging subject and master it. I am sufficiently confident in my own metacognitive abilities to think that I will be able to get through the boredom threshold of writing a book about an arguably quite boring subject.)

Back to Huang: if we can agree that student motivation must be the desire for mastery, what students should be demanding of a plenary is that it increases their powers of metacognition. Which is all very well. But, well … it leads us on to a question: Yeah, I've heard of it but, really, what is metacognition when it's at home?

A WORD ON META

Fascinatingly (and I mean, fascinatingly), the best definition I've brushed up against on this clever little prefix comes up with the following mind-blowing description: its use is to 'indicate a concept which is an abstraction from another concept'.[62] Which is exquisite. Though an abstraction from itself might be more accurate and might well be intellectually even more exquisite.

Its etymology is from the Greek preposition that indicates 'after', 'beyond' and 'adjacent', but also refers to the Greek word for 'self'. The Wikipedia entry goes on to describe it as meaning 'about (its own category)'. Consequently, a meta-analysis would be an analysis of an analysis; meta-art: art about art; a meta-comic would be a comic about the nature of comics; and one might reasonably argue that the book you are reading is, itself, meta-nothing.

---

62   Available at http://en.wikipedia.org/wiki/Meta (accessed 22 May 2013).

So metacognition is cognition about cognition *(knowledge about knowledge, thinking about thinking,*[63][64] or *knowing about knowing*[65]*)* and was previously thought by scientists to be 'a defining feature of human existence'[66] before they realised that rats were actually in some way conscious of whether they knew things or not. It was first defined by Flavell, whose definition is still held to be seminal:

> Metacognition refers to one's knowledge concerning one's own cognitive processes or anything related to them, e.g., the learning-relevant properties of information or data. For example, I am engaging in metacognition if I notice that I am having more trouble learning A than B; if it strikes me that I should double check C before accepting it as fact. Metacognition refers, amongst other things, to the active monitoring and consequent regulation and orchestration of these processes in relation to the cognitive objects on which they bear, usually in the form of some concrete goal or objective.[67]

It can quite easily be confused with cognition and there is a definite overlap. A relatively easy way of dealing with the abstraction comes from a paper by Garofalo and Lester entitled 'Metacognition, Cognitive Monitoring and

---

63 There is an account on Twitter wherein you can actually follow Twitter itself. Meta-twitter?

64 'Ah, but what about metamorphic rocks?' I hear you ask. 'How about the metatarsal?' In terms of chemistry, 'meta' is used either as a substitute for the Latin 'post', meaning 'after', or as an indication that something is in between two states. A metamorphic rock is neither one thing nor the other: it has gone through a change of form; the metatarsal is in between the phalanges and the tarsals: it's neither here nor there really, though tell that to Wayne Rooney. Actually don't. Wayne isn't at all interested in metacognition.

65 Janet Metcalfe and Arthur P. Shimamura, *Metacognition: Knowing about Knowing* (Cambridge, MA: MIT Press).

66 Allison L. Foote and Jonathon D Crystal, 'Metacognition in the Rat', *Current Biology* 17(6) (2007): 551–555, at 551.

67 John H. Flavell, 'Metacognitive Aspects of Problem Solving', in Lauren B. Resnick (ed.), *The Nature of Intelligence* (Hillsdale, NJ: Erlbaum), 231–236, at 232.

Mathematical Performance': 'Cognition is involved in doing, whereas meta-cognition is involved in choosing and planning what we do and monitoring what is being done.'[68] Rote learning, for instance, is a cognitive task as it involves the accretion of knowledge, but it is not in any way metacognitive. (Unless, of course, you are thinking how boring it is as you are doing it.)

There are three sub-sets to metacognition: *knowledge, experience(s)* and *regulation*.

1. METACOGNITIVE KNOWLEDGE

Flavell describes metacognitive knowledge as 'that segment of your (a child's, an adult's) stored world knowledge that has to do with people as cognitive creatures and with their diverse cognitive tasks, goals, actions, and experiences'.[69] He asserts that stored knowledge may be separated down into three factors that all interact with each other: *person, task* and *strategy*.

Metacognitive Knowledge about Person

Knowledge about person is what individuals know about themselves and about others in terms of their understanding of how learning works for them (and others). For instance, it is a piece of my own *intrapersonal* meta-cognitive knowledge that I write better with music on, but research better without it; and a further piece of metacognitive knowledge tells me I am at

---

68 Joe Garofalo and Frank K. Lester, 'Metacognition, Cognitive Monitoring and Mathematical Performance', *Journal for Research in Mathematics Education* 16 (1985): 163–176, at 164.
69 Flavell, 'Metacognition and Cognitive Monitoring', 906.

my very most fluent as a writer after half a bottle of Shiraz (or as I refer to it down the local Co-op, 'A bottle of metacognitive regulatory juice, please'). But I also have *interpersonal* metacognitive knowledge about my students. I am aware that Junior is inclined to give up if he doesn't understand things; that Farrell will ask to be spoonfed; that Steve is inclined to a slow start and has off days in which it is almost impossible to get him to do any work at all.

It is intrapersonal (arguably domain-specific) metacognitive knowledge that has helped me to write this book. From previous metacognitive experiences in writing books, I am aware that sitting and reading stuff off a screen, and then directly typing after I have read some source material or other, makes my writing a little lifeless, and skirts it too close to the source material. Metacognitively (intrapersonally), I am aware that merely cutting and pasting from your source materials is called plagiarism, or in publishing circles 'a Persaud', and that I'd be told off for doing so. Metacognitively (intrapersonally), I am aware that the better process, for me, is to print out loads of stuff, sit away from the computer reading it (perhaps even taking notes), process it and then go up to the computer half an hour later and see what belches out when I start engaging with the keyboard.

Metacognitive Knowledge about Task

Knowledge about task is specific to the activity in front of us, and is a series of relatively rapid judgements we might make about it. Is it difficult or easy? If it is difficult, then how difficult is it? Have we performed either this task before or a task that has some obvious relation to it? How might our previous knowledge of a related task help us? What strategies have we used previously that we might use on this task? What amount of time is it likely to take? Do we have enough information? Has it been sufficiently clearly explained? Do we know what is required of us? The metacognitive knowledge we have ascertained about the task will lead us towards the third variety of metacognitive knowledge.

Metacognitive Knowledge about Strategy

Strategising will lead on, hopefully inevitably, from our assessment of our task-related metacognitive knowledge, and our strategies might be broken down into goals and actions.

In terms of goals we might have an overarching objective to complete the task, but it may be that the best way of doing this is to break it down into a series of sub-goals (e.g. 'I'll get two pages done and then see where I am'). Once these sub-goals have been identified we enter the realm of strategy: using our prior metacognitive knowledge to establish whether it is time to use this strategy or that strategy. Flavell clarifies this with a simple example: 'The child may come to believe, for example, that one good way to learn and retain many bodies of information is to pay particular attention to the key points and try to repeat them to yourself in your own words.'[70] He is fairly emphatic about the influence of metacognitive knowledge on any learning encounter: 'It can lead you to select, evaluate, revise and abandon cognitive tasks.'[71]

There remains the question as to whether the strategies are activated consciously or unconsciously and whether this actually has any impact on their efficacy. Flavell talks about the differing kinds of activation of metacognitive

---

70 Flavell, 'Metacognition and Cognitive Monitoring', 907.
71 Flavell, 'Metacognition and Cognitive Monitoring', 908.

knowledge: 'A segment of it may be activated as the result of a deliberate, conscious memory search, for example for an effective strategy. On the other hand, and no doubt more commonly, the segment may be activated unintentionally and automatically by retrieval cues in the task situation.'[72] He goes on to pontificate about the success or failure of strategies whether they are consciously activated or not:

> However activated, it may and probably often does influence the course of the cognitive enterprise without itself entering consciousness. Alternatively, it may become or give rise to a conscious experience … Finally, and again like any other body of knowledge children acquire, it can be inaccurate, can fail to be activated when needed, can fail to have much or any influence when activated, and can fail to have a beneficial or adaptive effect when influential.[73]

Which all appears pretty difficult. In layman's bullet points, however, it becomes more simple:

- A metacognitive goal is made up of a series of sub-goals/actions that, when achieved, will, in combination, lead to completion of a (probably complex) task.

- Metacognitive strategies are employed after we've set goals, and are the processes we've selected by which we will go about performing or undertaking the task.

- These strategies can be searched for consciously, but it is more likely they will just come to us unconsciously.

- Sometimes it doesn't matter what process you go through – conscious or unconscious – nothing works.

---

72 Flavell, 'Metacognition and Cognitive Monitoring', 907.
73 Flavell, 'Metacognition and Cognitive Monitoring', 907–908.

2. METACOGNITIVE EXPERIENCE(S)

Any cognitive task you have ever undertaken is, or should be (or contain), a metacognitive experience. During the completion of the task you will, at some point, have been caused to start thinking about the process of doing it: you will have been puzzled, you may have been bored.

Student: I'm bored of doing this, sir.

Teacher: No, you're not. You are having a mildly negative metacognitive experience.

Student: Huh?

Even giving up on the task because it is too hard and chucking your flailing exercise book towards the corner of the room in a fit of pique is a metacognitive experience. Likewise, having a moment of revelation, an 'Aha' moment, where it all comes together as you think about (or, as is more likely, don't think about) the task. Even thinking, 'God, I've still got five pages of this bloody essay to go' is a metacognitive experience.

It appears that this concept can be separated into two, and that one sub-category is a fissile element which almost goes so far as to hint at the metaphysical: a metacognitive experience is not only any cognitive task (experienced as an overarching narrative), but through the process of being involved in any metacognitive narrative, there are also moments of profound and blinding metacognitive epiphany, which might themselves also be termed experience(s). These are any experiences (which may or may not be related to the current endeavour) that have somehow, ultimately, affected or adapted the metacognitive knowledge of the individual.

One of the ways I put bacon on the family table is taking GCSE English Language students through what I (and now others) call the 'walking talking mock'. This is something I invented while teaching in a school in Coulsdon, and which the PiXL Club have appropriated and used more or less successfully.[74] I take a whole year group into a draughty hall and make them wish opposable thumbs had never evolved. This specific exam is more a (really very testing) time management exercise than it is in any way an intellectually taxing one, and the issue with students sitting this exam for the first time when they are actually in the high stakes situation of the GCSE proper is that they have not had sufficient metacognitive *experience* of this sort of thing to have the *strategic* metacognitive *knowledge* of how to perform as well as they might. In going through the paper and telling them exactly at what point they must stop each question, how long they must plan for their next answer, at what point they have to start the next question and for how long they must write it, we develop their metacognitive knowledge of how to perform best at this particular exam when the real thing comes along. Metacognitive experience is therefore the training that students must put themselves (or be put) through in order to be properly rehearsed when high stakes situations come about. Related to this, any metacognitive experience that you give your students might be compared to the regime that footballers, for instance, go through where they rehearse the same movement time after time in order to develop what they describe as 'muscle memory'. Metacognitive knowledge is the muscle memory itself, though in this case the muscle in question is the brain.

It's obvious here that any metacognitive experience must, inevitably, affect the other two forms of metacognition. The plenary is, by definition, a metacognitive experience, and our intention as serious practitioners might be to help develop our students' future metacognitive regulation and increase their metacognitive knowledge.

---

74   The PiXL Club is a school leaders' association: http://www.pixl.org.uk/.

3. METACOGNITIVE REGULATION

Metacognitive regulation is the process by which people exert control over themselves and their responses when they are undertaking learning experiences: how they monitor their own process of creating and retaining memory; how they regulate their behaviour so that they maximise their potential and are in their own particular optimum state for learning. This can be as simple as just convincing yourself to remain focused or becoming aware that you are in need of a break because the information is not going into your head any more.

The various skills of self-regulation are reported, perhaps over-simplistically, as being threefold: *planning*, *monitoring* and *regulating*.

Planning

Planning includes activities such as setting goals for studying, skimming a text before reading it and coming up with a set of questions you might want answered before reading a text. Flavell writes: 'Skimming a set of directions to get a rough idea of how hard they are going to be to follow or remember is a metacognitive strategy.'[75] These activities help students plan their use of metacognitive strategies, activate prior knowledge and organise and comprehend materials. It has been argued that people with metacognitive knowledge are able to see the block in the road coming and are able to do something about it; they will have planned for the variable outcomes that might occur in the messy, non-zero-sum game of learning. A metacognitive planner will have been involved in a process of metacognition before undertaking a learning task: they will have planned for it. They may have asked

---

75   Flavell, 'Metacognition and Cognitive Monitoring', 909.

themselves what previously acquired skills or pieces of knowledge might help with the oncoming task. They may have thought about what their goal is: what they actually want to learn. Finally, they may have a strategy for what they are going to do first and what they will do if they get stuck.

One of the bosses of 'this sort of thing', Marsha Lovett, quoting a study from Azevedo and Cromley, lists five key parts to planning:[76]

1   Time and effort planning

2   Prior knowledge activation

3   Goal-directed search

4   Evaluating content as an answer to the current goal

5   Reminding themselves of the current goal

How might these look in a classroom? Is it possible to create a proforma that students might be able to use at the beginning of their understanding of metacognition? Let's see.

The following table might profitably be used when setting a research home-work task or as a starter activity to complete before performing a task, and to have as a useful reference document during the task. It will certainly encourage students to develop their skills of metacognitive regulation. As a classwork task, it is perhaps best employed with older students, as they have to contemplate the idea of taking a break during the lesson, and this may be something that requires maturity, otherwise the break will go on till, erm, break.

---

76   Marsha C. Lovett, 'Teaching Metacognition'. Presentation to the Educause Learning Initiative Annual Meeting, 29 January 2008, citing Roger Azevedo and Jennifer G. Cromley, 'Does Training on Self-Regulated Learning Facilitate Students' Learning with Hypermedia?' *Journal of Educational Psychology* 96(3) (2004): 523–535.

Metacognitive regulation: planning proforma

Metacognitive area	Key questions	
Time and effort planning	How long are you going to spend on this task? How are you going to ensure that you maximise your effort? Will you take a break at any point? If so, when and why?	
Prior knowledge activation	What do you already know about this subject that is somehow relevant to the current endeavour?	
Goal-directed search	What are you looking for? And where are you going to find it? What is your back-up plan if you cannot find what you are looking for?	
Evaluating content as an answer to the current goal	How will you know (or what process will you use) that the information you have located is relevant to your learning goal?	

Metacognitive area	Key questions	
Reminding yourself of the current goal	How are you going to ensure that you remain on task? At what stage will you notice that you are going off on a tangent? What are your key triggers or indicators that you are going off task?	

Monitoring

Monitoring activities include checking yourself to ensure that you are paying proper attention when either reading a text or listening to a lecture: for instance, asking questions of yourself about your levels of comprehension or focus during the learning event, or monitoring your comprehension of a lecture. During a task – and provided we are not in flow state – we will have a continual inner monologue about how it is going; we will monitor our own progress, tell ourselves to keep going, suppress impulsive behaviour or, alternatively, give in to it and admit it's time to give up. All of these are part of a process of metacognitive monitoring.[77]

---

77 There is some doubt, however, as to how useful these questions might actually be, and Flavell sounds a note of warning: 'Might it not even do more harm than good, especially if used in excess or nonselectively? Think of the feckless obsessive, paralysed by incessant critical evaluation of his own judgements and decisions' (Flavell, 'Metacognition and Cognitive Monitoring').

Regulation

Regulation strategies are what you use when your monitoring activities have revealed that you've 'gone off the boil' to bring your behaviour back to the point where you are achieving whatever goal you have for the learning experience. Regulation is self-correcting behaviour that occurs as a result of monitoring.

'These three varieties of metacognitive strategies improve learning by helping students correct their studying behavior as they are going along and help them to consciously repair deficits in their understanding.'[78]

SELF-REGULATION, OVER-LEARNING AND SWIMMING

The intention is that students will reach automaticity, and that they might do this through a process of over-learning. Hattie describes this concept with reference to elite swimmers:

> To reach a state of over-learning requires much deliberate practice – that is, extensive engagement in relevant practice activities for improving performance (as when swimmers swim lap after lap aiming to over-learn the key aspects of their strokes, turns, and breathing). It is not deliberate practice for the sake of repetitive training, but deliberate practice focused on improving particular aspects of performance, to better understand how to monitor, self-regulate, and evaluate one's performance, and to reduce errors.[79]

78 Huang et al., 'Building an E-Portfolio Learning Model', 21.
79 Hattie, *Visible Learning for Teachers*, 18.

Indeed, swimming coaches regard the skills of self-regulation as vital to the success (or not) of the athlete: 'Athletes who fail to self-regulate are less disciplined and motivated, show less initiative, and fail to maximise opportunities for acquisition during training.'[80]

Athletes eventually grow away from their coaches and make decisions independently of them. When independent of the coach they must rely on self-regulation. A teacher is more or less a coach to, in some cases, a very large group of young people and, like a coach, should be providing opportunities for their students to develop their self-regulated behaviours in order to be responsible for their own learning. You can argue, then, that explicit and regular practice at metacognitive strategies will lead our students to automaticity in this area, and will further lead them, like the practised swimmer, to be able to focus on the various nuances of self-regulation so that they may become fully rounded performers who are adept at specifically focusing on elements of their cognition; improvement in which is a prerequisite to them bettering their previous personal bests.

Which is where (I hope) Part 4 of this book comes in.

---

80 Bradley W. Young and Janet L. Starkes, 'Coaches' Perceptions of Non-Regulated Training Behaviors in Competitive Swimmers', *International Journal of Sports Science and Coaching* 1 (2006): 53–68.

PART 4
DIGITAL PLENARIES

The sharper reader might identify a jarring paradox over these next several pages. This section has been entitled 'Digital Plenaries' because its intent is to come up with a series of plenary options that are based around what Professor John Hattie's meta-analysis[81] has told us are the most effective strategies for teaching in terms of effect size: it is this section of the book that is meant to be the most topical and will incorporate the most recent findings. As it is meant to be bang up to date, cutting edge and so on, I've given it the epithet 'digital' to delude both you, poor reader, and myself into the belief that what you have here is at the razor sharp cutting edge of modernity.

In the process of writing it, however, and looking into the shallows of the research, something strange and upsetting has occurred: I've realised that pretty well all the strategies that Hattie suggests have a beneficial effect size are old fashioned to the point of seeming as if they were decayed at the point Noah first noticed the air felt a little moist. My analysis of this (should you be in the least bit interested) is less obvious and less reactionary than you might think. The traditionalist might argue gleefully that Hattie's research proves that 'traditional methods work', to coin a phrase that some right-wing commentator might once have scribed on a now discontinued blog for the *Daily Telegraph*. But I suspect that the answer is a little less crass and a little more worrying in the grand scheme of things.

---

81 Hattie, *Visible Learning*.

Despite the consistent government pressure, down-talking, witch-hunting, nay-saying, league-tabling and teacher-persecuting discourse about schools that populates a proudly ignorant media's coverage of the British education system's achievements, you only have to read the first page of any renowned American educator's thoughts on the art of teaching and learning to come to the pretty firm and certain realisation that British educators are, at the very least, twenty years ahead of our former colony in terms of moving the art form forward.

Much of the research that Hattie has meta-analysed has come from the United States; one might argue, therefore, that he is dealing with a hand of cards that contains rather too many deuces. If we start out from the admittedly controversial and arguably offensive assumption that Americans don't know a great deal about progressive approaches to teaching and learning, then we might easily take a further jump towards the conclusion that the best of their techniques, when judged against their other less successful techniques, are still just a little bit rubbish. There is a further argument that the meta-analysis has been of every study that Hattie's team could get their hands on, and that these would go back for donkey's years. Consequently, the evidence base includes a hell of a lot of very old-fashioned stuff and not much that is in any way new. Such is the nature of the longitudes of time.

This section of the book is constructed with reference to one of the sections of *Visible Learning* in which Hattie quotes a piece of research from an unpublished PhD thesis by Lynn Lavery, in which the various self-regulatory strategies are evaluated and an effect size is attributed to them.[82] For the purpose of this book, which is to equip you with the most effective strategies for your students' retention of learning, we will look at those which are attributed an effect size of over 0.4 (which is the effect size Hattie suggests is in the area we want to be in order to affect real, unarguable learning gains).

---

82 Lynn Lavery, 'Self-Regulated Learning for Academic Success: An Evaluation of Instructional Techniques', unpublished PhD thesis, University of Auckland, 2008.

Various metacognitive strategies and the effect sizes

Strategy	Definition	Description	No. of effects	Effect size
Organising and transforming	Overt or covert rearrangement of instructional materials to improve learning	Making an outline before writing a paper	89	0.85
Self-consequences	Student arrangement or imagination of rewards or punishment for success or failure	Putting off pleasurable events until work is completed	75	0.70
Self-instruction	Self-verbalising the steps to complete a given task	Verbalising steps in solving a maths problem	124	0.62
Self-evaluation	Setting standards and using them for self-judgement	Checking work before handing in to teacher	156	0.62

Strategy	Definition	Description	No. of effects	Effect size
Help-seeking	Efforts to seek help from either a peer, teacher or other adult	Using a study partner	62	0.60
Keeping records	Recording of information related to study tasks	Taking class notes	46	0.59
Rehearsing and memorising	Memorisation of material by overt or covert strategies	Writing down a mathematics formula until it is remembered	99	0.57
Goal-setting/ planning	Setting of educational goals or planning of sub-goals and planning for sequencing, timing and completing activities related to those goals	Making lists to accomplish during study	130	0.49

Strategy	Definition	Description	No. of effects	Effect size
Reviewing records	Efforts to reread notes, tests or textbooks to prepare for class or further testing	Reviewing class textbook before going to lecture	131	0.49
Self-monitoring	Observing and tracking one's own performance and actions, often recording them	Keeping records of study output	154	0.45
Task strategies	Analysing tasks and identifying specific, advantageous methods for learning	Creating mnemonics to remember facts	154	0.45
Imagery	Creating or recalling vivid mental images to assist learning	Imagining the consequences of failing to study	6	0.44

Strategy	Definition	Description	No. of effects	Effect size
Time management	Estimating and budgeting use of time	Scheduling daily studying and homework time	8	0.44

Source: John Hattie, *Visible Learning: A Synthesis of over 800 Meta-Analyses Relating to Achievement* (Abingdon: Routledge, 2009), Table 9.5, at 190.

We'll now take them from the top down, suggesting ways in which you might arrange specifically metacognitive plenary tasks to improve your students' knowledge retention.

1. HOMEWORK'S HOLY GRAIL

Everyday, millions of innocent children are unwillingly part of a terrible dictatorship. The government takes them away from their families and brings them to cramped, crowded buildings where they are treated as slaves in terrible conditions. For seven hours a day, they are indoctrinated to love their current conditions and support their government and society. As if this was not enough, they are often held for another two hours to exert themselves almost to the point of physical exhaustion, and sometimes injury. Then, when at home, during the short few hours which they are permitted to see their families they are forced to do additional mind-numbing work which they finish and return the following day.[83]

Homework need not necessarily be mind-numbing, it need not be off the top of your head and need not necessarily be just a badly photocopied piece of paper that you haven't read (and so don't realise it has no supporting logic nor indeed any educational value). It seems perhaps eccentric, but there's a lot of mileage in homework being used as a metacognitive task. If we go back to Hattie's previously cited line about feedback from students to teachers, then there is a solid argument for setting homework tasks that are in some way an evaluation of the learning that has, or has not, taken place. Here we are in the arena of the easily constructed proforma.

---

83   Speech by Aaron Swartz at school assembly (at age 14).

Homework – Evaluating the lesson	
Can you identify what you were meant to learn in the last lesson?	
Did you learn anything else unexpected?	
What was the most successful aspect of the lesson for you?	
What aspects of the lesson would you have changed if you were to make it more successful for future classes?	
Is there any information that you feel you still need to properly understand this lesson's subject matter more fully?	

Of course, this proforma (or your own, far better version of it) can just as easily be used at the end of the lesson as it can as a homework task. The benefits to having it as a plenary activity would be that you can take the answers in at the end of the lesson and use these as a planning device for the next lesson, as you now know what the kids feel they need to know next and don't just have to guess, mark their work searching for it or act on unsupported hunches.

There are other ideas that could be used to make homework profitably meta-cognitive. Ask students to design an activity with which they would test the learning of the lesson for homework, and then, the next session, ask them to perform their own activity or a series of activities that are an agglomeration of the best ideas the class have had for the previous homework.

2. ORGANISING AND TRANSFORMING

Organising and transforming	Overt or covert rearrangement of instructional materials to improve learning	Making an outline before writing a paper

Source: John Hattie, *Visible Learning: A Synthesis of over 800 Meta-Analyses Relating to Achievement* (Abingdon: Routledge, 2009), Table 9.5, at 190.

Whilst the research above gives a kind of proactive example in which a response is planned, we are at the 'endy' bit of the lesson and so any organising or transforming activities necessarily have to be reactive to the learning that has (or has not) taken place.

Here we bear in mind the advice we give to students whose approach to revision is to sit in front of a textbook, sweating, willing the information to go into their heads and finding that they have read the same sentence twenty times without any cognition or learning occurring. Time has passed. Nothing has changed. We advise them to do something with the information: to reprocess it in some form. That way it is more likely, through the process of having done something active with it, to stay in the head.

We can bring to bear the many millions[84] of active learning techniques outlined by Geoff Petty. The following are from his '25 Ways for Teaching without Talking'.[85]

- **Key points:** Give them a piece of text related to the learning and get them to decide what they think is the key point from the learning.

- **Highlighting:** As above with a highlighter pen or two.

- **Transformation:** You take the information from one form into another: from note form into essay form, essay form into note form; list of key points into song lyric, song lyric into list of key points; chronological time frame into a list ordered into importance, list ordered in importance into chronological, etc.

- **Headings:** Give the information from the lesson and ask students to group this into headings. These can be defined or (more interestingly) left for them to design. It's useful to provide an empty tabular proforma and a glue stick.

---

84 In fact millions.

85 Geoff Petty, '25 Ways for Teaching without Talking: Presenting Students with New Material in Theory Lessons' (2002). Available at http://geoffpetty.com/wp-content/uploads/2012/12/25waysforTWT2.doc (accessed 22 May 2013).

3. SELF-CONSEQUENCES AND 13. IMAGERY

Self-consequences	Student arrangement or imagination of rewards or punishment for success or failure	Putting off pleasurable events until work is completed
Imagery	Creating or recalling vivid mental images to assist learning	Imagining the consequences of failing to study

Source: John Hattie, *Visible Learning: A Synthesis of over 800 Meta-Analyses Relating to Achievement* (Abingdon: Routledge, 2009), Table 9.5, at 190.

According to one theory learning is brought about by conditioning, that is, by systematic reward of the desired responses and punishment of the unwanted ones. By this method pigeons can be taught complex skills and rats learn to run complicated mazes. Conditioning techniques are successful in teaching a wide variety of skills and attitudes.[86]

There is an apparent absurdity here, a temptation towards feeling foolish that might cause us to discount the possibility of using this potentially valuable tool. But if we are to take the work of the man whose name bears

---

86   Broudy, 'The Role of Imagery in Learning', 8.

relation to an adjective that might be used to describe someone who wears hats as an innate part of their personality[87] with the degree of seriousness and reverence we are told we must, then 'the research says' we have a responsibility to overcome our innate sense of absurdity and instruct our students to involve themselves in this process.

Daniel Goleman describes the ability to control impulse as the 'master aptitude'.[88] Let's go further with this. There is one ethnicity that, no matter where they live, no matter in which country or city they find themselves – be it Brazil, Botswana, Bahrain, Bromley or Beijing – they always nestle at the very top of the league tables of educational attainment. The ethnicity? The Chinese, of course. The reason? Well, it's simple: they work harder than anyone else.

A white working class student might come home to be asked by his father how he is doing in maths. He might reply, 'Not well, Dad. I'm not good at maths,' only to be greeted with the response, 'That's alright son, you're good at English. No one needs to be good at everything.' A Chinese student in the same situation, who is struggling with a particular subject, might be encouraged to get up at stupid-o-clock in the morning to study the subject in which they are struggling. Leaving racist clichés aside though, and acknowledging that the educational achievements of Southeast Asians are built on the backs of the corpses of the failures,[89] it might be worth engaging with this in a more benign way.

---

87 Hattie. Geddit?

88 Daniel Goleman, *Emotional Intelligence: Why It Can Matter More Than IQ* (London: Bloomsbury, 1995), 78.

89 A former East Asia correspondent for the *Washington Post*, Blaine Harden, says: 'South Koreans work more, sleep less and kill themselves at a higher rate than citizens of any other developed country. Self-worth tends to be narrowly defined by admission to a few selected universities.' Read more in my article of the *Sydney Morning Herald* 'High Scores Come At a Higher Cost. Available at http://www.smh.com.au/opinion/politics/high-scores-come-at-a-higher-cost-20120729-2365e.html#ixzz2A9cUMiEK (accessed 22 May 2013).

Imagine a reward: relate the learning to that reward. It may be that just such an (apparently crass) visualisation exercise will put student into the 'Mo Farah mindset'. It can be done! It can be learnt! Alternatively, it might be less intellectually facile to ask kids at the end of the lesson to write down what their intended goal in terms of career is, and then attempt to relate the learning of the lesson to that intended goal (which is more interesting and more valid than it might initially seem). (For confirmation of this refer back to the 'Show Me the Money' analogue plenary on page 44.)

The obverse of this is that you have classes full of children imagining the punishment they might be in receipt of should they not learn what is on their plate. Which is a divertingly Dickensian image. One might even go so far as to construct an imaginary landscape of Bosch-like medieval tortures that they must visualise if they do not learn the information of the lesson. If you do not have this information in your head by the end of the lesson you will be coated in honey and licked to death by aardvarks. Or we could go further and plaster a frieze of Bosch's *The Garden of Earthly Delights* on the wall, point the students in the direction of a horrific tableau and inform them gravely that if they do not embed this lesson's learning in their heads, then it is more than likely that they will be condemned to having a flute (that spits coins) permanently lodged up their fundament. Focus children!

On a related (though academically) distinct subject, the role of imagery in learning goes all the way back to the early seventeenth century and a Moravian teacher called John Amos Comenius who championed universal education and who also, in *Didactica Magna* (Great Didactic), invented the organisational system that Americans use to this day: kindergarten, elementary school, secondary school, college and university. His lasting pedagogical influence, however, was in being the first teacher to use pictures as aids in language learning. Hs textbooks started off with simple concepts that the child would be able to relate to, which were written – predominantly – in the home language rather than the language being learnt, and then illustrated.

It is off the base of Comenius that others have taken the half-leap towards examining the role of imagery.

One of the more interesting of these is Allan Paivio's dual-coding theory, which runs nicely up against the theories of lateralisation of brain function and suggests that we have two distinct (though correlated) systems for encoding, retaining and retracting knowledge: the visual and the verbal. The word *rabbit*, for instance, has two reverberations. If you can just focus on the italicised vermin in the above sentence for a couple of seconds, please. You are, by looking at the word, thinking about a rabbit. The platonic essence of rabbit is, therefore, stored in your mind as being related to the sequence of letters that signify it. You may also find that by looking at the letters a picture of Bugs Bunny or one of his less verbose cousins comes into your head; which, though a picture, and therefore giving the impression of the real thing more closely than the letters, is still merely a signifier of rabbit. You therefore have two systems to retain the knowledge of what a rabbit is: linguistic and pictorial.

But there's more – dual-coding theory has it that there are three representative systems:

- **Representational:** where verbal or non-verbal representations are directly activated.

- **Referential:** where the verbal system activates the imagistic system (see the word rabbit, picture a rabbit in your head) or where the imagistic system activates the verbal (see a picture of a rabbit, think of the word rabbit).

- **Associative processing:** where representations are activated solely within either system (the word rabbit makes you think of the word hare; a picture of a rabbit makes you picture its wild-eyed cousin with the bigger ears and the longer levers).

Paivio concludes that our perceiving of what is in front of us will always contain a mix of all three kinds of processing; and that we perceive through both logogens – the information that lies beneath our understanding of a word – and imagens – the various constituent parts of an image. According to him, 'Imagery is centrally important in facilitating long-term retention, at least for adults.'[90]

This leads us towards the work of Bull and Wittrock, who experimented with three separate classes of students and a set of eighteen nouns: they set up an experiment in which they would use different methods to teach the kids the definition/meaning of those nouns. One class had to create what is described as 'self-generated imagery', another had 'given imagery' and a further class just had the verbal definitions. And here we are in the region of the reveal shot; the 'guess who did best' children. I'll let you theorise about this briefly before you start reading the following quote (which will give you the answer):

> The verbal definition group or control group was told to learn each definition by reading the words and writing them down repeatedly during the allotted interval. The 'imagery given' group received words, definitions and illustrations. They were instructed to read the word and definition and then write it down once and then to trace its picture. The 'image discovery' [group] was to follow the instructions given to the second group but instead of tracing the given illustration were to draw a pictorial representation of the word and its definitions. It was found after due respect to statistical cautions that the retention rate was better when 10-year-old children 'discovered and drew idiosyncratic images to represent nouns and their verbal definitions'.[91]

---

90 Allan Paivio, *Imagery and Verbal Processes* (New York: Holt, Rinehart, and Winston), 327–332.
91 Britta L. Bull and Merlin C. Wittrock, 'Imagery in the Learning of Verbal Definitions', *British Journal of Educational Psychology* 43(3) (1973): 289–293, at 289.

Bull and Wittrock give us empirical confirmation of something teachers since the time of Comenius have always suspected: that using imagery for learning language is a useful technique. So, where does this fit in with a book about the plenary? I recommended a technique a few books ago for a plenary in which you merely ask students to draw the learning that has taken place, and have been in receipt of a few e-mails from teachers saying it didn't work. My reply to these teachers was that – as with all new things – you've got to give it time. If a new teaching technique doesn't work the first time, then you have to commit to do it another three times at least. If it doesn't work after practice and review, then perhaps it isn't a great idea. The idea of students drawing the learning (particularly if this is in an idiosyncratic or surreal way) and then showing their drawing to at least three other people and explaining, after the others have attempted to interpret it, how it embodies the learning, fits well with the research of Bull and Wittrock. As a technique it stands on the shoulders of giants such as Comenius. Try it four times. Ask the kids to attempt to memorise their drawings, and they will be memorising the learning.

4. SELF-INSTRUCTION

Self-instruction	Self-verbalising the steps to complete a given task	Verbalising steps in solving a maths problem

Source: John Hattie, *Visible Learning: A Synthesis of over 800 Meta-Analyses Relating to Achievement* (Abingdon: Routledge, 2009), Table 9.5, at 190.

This appears an initially promising idea that fits with current notions of independent learning and developing our students into self-directed autodidacts who will eventually develop, like the bailiff's clerk in Sartre's *Nausea*, into the kind of people who go to the local library to read their way through all the books therein in alphabetical order. Sadly, it isn't as promising as the title makes it appear.

On investigation, it is merely a set of easy-to-follow instructions seemingly targeted at teaching the mentally infirm to perform the most basic of tasks. Briefly, the principle is that you are shown/modelled a task, which you then perform, all the while narrating what you are doing.

The steps of self-instruction are:

1   Teacher models task while saying it out loud.

2   Student performs the task while the teacher says the steps out loud.

3   Student performs the task while saying the steps out loud.

Self-instruction originally appears to be the kind of learning strategy that will land you in receipt of anxious looks from your fellow passengers on life's omnibus, as a key part of it is that you employ self-talk and must (apparently) say it out loud: 'Self-instruction involves a person telling him or herself to do something and then doing it.'[92] Whilst it is said to be an 'un-obtrusive self-management tool',[93] you can liken it to the commentating-on-your-own-life that seven-year-old boys, 1970s PE teachers and overpaid, balding mockney educationalists indulge themselves in: 'I am going to get on the bus, and then when I have got on the bus I am going to pay the bus driver with all my one penny coins, and then I am going to tell the person who is listening in to my self-instruction thinking that I am mad, who is immediately behind me in the bus queue as I am saying this, to desist from being a nosey swine ...'

In truth, this is a learning strategy suited perhaps only to the beginning of the lesson and, furthermore, is vastly more suited to learning a series of basic steps than assimilating any abstract or complex idea. You can imagine it working with learning to cook a workable soft-boiled egg; embedding complex thought is a bigger ask. However, we will attempt to use it as a basis for a riff that might work as a usable plenary.

---

92 Carolyn Hughes, 'Self-Instruction', in Martin Agran (ed.), *Student-Directed Learning: Teaching Self-Determination Skills* (Detroit, MI: Brooks/Cole, 1997), 144–170, at 146.

93 Michael L. Wehmeyer, 'Self-Instruction'. Available at http://www.dps.missouri.edu/resources/MoreThanAJob/Supports/Supports%202/02%20Self-Instruction.htm (accessed 22 May 2013).

Blown up a little into more detailed relief we can use the five steps, as identified by Wehmeyer, Agran and Hughes in 1998,[94] which are:

- Step 1: Identify the problem. If we relocate this to the plenary task, then the problem must be that we want to embed the learning from the lesson into our heads.

- Step 2: Identify a possible response to the problem. Here the students will have to get creative and we are, potentially, beyond the realms of 'self-instruction-as-being-the-kind-of-intellectually-facile-nonsense-that-academics-come-up-with-that-teachers-know-will-not-work-in-a-classroom-for-it-is-plainly-too-stupid' and into the realms of the, 'Erm, well just maybe there is some mileage in this apparent non-idea'. The student has to identify the strategy with which they might best remember the information in the lesson. Here, if we have attacked the idea of the metacognitive plenary with some kind of a plan, then the students might well have a range of strategies they can employ and from which they will select. They will, at this point, be involved in metacognitive self-regulation as they will be picking a strategy that works for them.

- Step 3: Evaluate the response. Having identified the strategy they are going to use to embed the knowledge, they must evaluate whether it is likely to have worked: to verbalise the question, 'Did it work?', and to articulate their responses to that question. It is probably better here that they pair up and ask each other questions as this technique really does feel too much like entering the realms of the mentally unbalanced if you have a whole classroom of children sitting on their own and asking themselves questions out loud, and then answering themselves!

---

94 Michael L. Wehmeyer, Martin Agran and Carolyn Hughes, 'Teaching Self-Instruction Skills', in *eidem*, *Teaching Self-Determination to Students with Disabilities: Basic Skills for Successful Transition* (Baltimore, MD: Paul H. Brookes, 1998), 157–183.

- Step 4: Self-reinforce. The existence of this stage is a satire of itself.[95] But the idea is that they must then come up with a superlative and congratulate themselves on learning the information in the lesson, or at least acknowledge, verbally, that they performed the task, what that task was and what the intent of it was.

- Step 5: Train the behaviour to match verbal statements. This, if we are talking about plenaries, would be the part of the sequence that is reactivated when the next self-instruction plenary is used. When we start off the next plenary, probably best in the next lesson, students must be asked to recall the sequence of the last plenary. You can talk this out or map it onto the whiteboard so that the stages are explicit. If you perform another self-instruction plenary, then hopefully this will be a technique that will then become trained behaviour and all you will have to do in future is ask students to conduct a self-instruction plenary.

There is a further even more dribble-specked variant to self-instruction: did–next–now. You state, again out loud, the step you've completed (*did*), then state out loud the step you've got to do next (*next*). Finally, you state, yet again out loud, what you are going to do now (*now*).

At the end of each stage it's genuinely recommended that the poor person performing the task states out loud, 'I did what I said I'd do'. Clearly, this is a strategy you might employ to teach a buck-toothed waffle waitress who is kissing cousins with a spectacularly unintelligent monkey how to lay a table, but this does not stop it being the subject of serious academic study, or being regarded by those serious academics as having a large effect size.

---

95 Though it might work in pairs.

5. SELF-EVALUATION

Self-evaluation	Setting standards and using them for self-judgement	Checking work before handing in to teacher

Source: John Hattie, *Visible Learning: A Synthesis of over 800 Meta-Analyses Relating to Achievement* (Abingdon: Routledge, 2009), Table 9.5, at 190.

The best path through self-evaluation is clearly self-assessment (or peer assessment) in which the student examines their own work alongside a set of assessment criteria, either provided by an exam board or in the form of three things written rapidly on the board by the teacher who is grasping desperately for a workable plenary. The only thing I have to add here to the work of people who are experts in this realm (one of which I am definitely not) is an idea from boys' achievement expert, Garry Wilson: if you want a student to self-assess a piece of work they have just spent half an hour doing, give them a minute's break before they have to do it. Let them walk around the room and have a brief chat with a mate, so that they come back to it a little fresher.

There are varieties of grouping and feedback that can be used in this instance:

1   Self-assessment then grouped discussion.

2   Self-assessment then paired discussion.

3   Self-assessment then written targets for future improvement.

4   Peer assessment then paired discussion.

5   Peer assessment then written feedback.

6. HELP-SEEKING

Help-seeking	Efforts to seek help from either a peer, teacher or other adult	Using a study partner

Source: John Hattie, *Visible Learning: A Synthesis of over 800 Meta-Analyses Relating to Achievement* (Abingdon: Routledge, 2009), Table 9.5, at 190.

There are ten pages of enormously well thought out and really useful advice on the subject of help-seeking in Jim Smith's *Follow Me, I'm Right Behind You: Whole School Progress the Lazy Way*. The best of these is instituting a 3B4ME policy in class, wherein students in need of help have to try out at least three different strategies to get them unstuck before they can access the over-busy resource of the teacher. One could institute this as students having to ask three other people in the class before speaking to the teacher as a policy related to help-seeking in class.

Jim's battery of strategies related to help-seeking are well worth a look in the context of their natural environment,[96] but with his permission I'll bowdlerise and plagiarise, as his ideas are better than mine on this subject.

1   Imagine you are someone else. Put yourself in their character and imagine how they might go about ensuring that the information from the lesson sticks in their head.

---

96   This is a plug. *Whole School Progress the Lazy Way* is very much one of the better pieces of thinking about teaching released over the last few years.

2   Ask the students to identify what have they forgotten from this lesson. Which seems a tangential and arguably nonsensical approach to a plenary, but there is method in it. In searching for the information that they have been in reception of, but have arguably forgotten, they are forced to think quite hard, to 'dig deep' about the learning of the lesson.

3   Have students identified as progress coaches. This is lazy teaching to the point of being really rather slack! Rather than have any involvement at all with the plenary, the teacher nominates five or six kids in the class, gives them a patronising, laminated badge emblazoned with the phrase 'Teacher's Little Helper', 'Elf', 'Dupe' or 'Progress Leader', whichever is most likely to obtain buy-in. Come the last ten minutes, students should approach the progress leaders with whatever questions they have about the learning from the lesson. The teacher may take a nap at this point.

4   The Wall of Independence. This is a genuinely marvellous idea: you nominate a surface within the classroom and cover it with whatever material your creativity leads you to. Throughout the process/progress of the lesson, students record questions that have occurred to them about the learning on the wall. For the plenary, you either get the students to answer them on the wall or simply review all the questions and answers, discussing them as a class as you do so.

7. KEEPING RECORDS

Keeping records	Recording of information related to study tasks	Taking class notes

Source: John Hattie, *Visible Learning: A Synthesis of over 800 Meta-Analyses Relating to Achievement* (Abingdon: Routledge, 2009), Table 9.5, at 190.

I don't know if you have ever launched into a far-too-speaky lesson and asked the students to take notes; whenever I have done so I've been greeted with looks of utter incomprehension. 'What can he ever mean? What is this "taking notes" of which he speaks? I cannot say that I have ever encountered this concept. Surely, he is – as ever – making it all up as he goes along.'

If you think back to your own education it is difficult to pin down the point at which you learnt to takes notes: was it during your A levels? Perhaps sooner, perhaps not. You may be able to remember if it is nearer for you, but as this writer is now approaching the later stages of the middle years, it is now so long ago that I learnt to take notes that I have no idea when it was. What is apparent, though, is that it is possibly unlikely that your own students will *not* know how to take them[97] and that you may as well be the one who teaches them this potentially useful life skill. (When's a good time to do this? How about now?)

---

97   If you doubt this, ask them tomorrow. See what happens.

Firstly, why is note-taking valuable or useful? There will have been times during your own academic career when you noticed (probably while copying up your own notes at university) that it is actually a barely cognitive task, and seems to revolve predominantly around making the scruffy handwriting look prettier by either typing it up or writing it out in 'neat', which is not that complex a skill, and clearly has you working a long way short of your personal zone of proximal development.

In answer to this, the first reason is that note-taking is a means of remaining focused and in the moment when you are being spoken at. We are prone to drifting off when in a situation that requires us to focus for overly long periods on someone speaking or presenting. Taking notes is a device that operates as a prompt to focusing. (In taking notes you are also encouraging the teacher, sending them a message that you are on task and are in some way engaged.)

Note-taking makes you an active part of the learning, rather than the passive participant letting the lecture wash blithely over you. It is a mechanism for thought capture: you can record and organise your ideas about a certain subject; your queries; the things you have decided that you have to do to follow up the lecture. You can permanently capture content that would otherwise be entirely ephemeral. You can also process this content at a later point by reviewing your notes, and this is where we enter the realms of their potential value as a plenary activity. You, as teacher, might ask your students to review their notes at the end of the lesson and to share this review with other students, noting the queries they have raised and seeing if they can solve those questions together. It may be that you can bash this up against the notion of spaced repetition as a homework task that can also serve the function of a plenary. If we look back to David Cox's suggestions (see Analogue Plenary 21: Spaced Repetition), we can see that it would be possible to set a plenary task to review your notes: this evening (Monday) after school, tomorrow evening (Tuesday) after school and on Friday evening. There will be a test next Monday.

There is a further benefit to analogue note-taking as has been touched upon briefly in the section on metacognitive knowledge. New technologies bring not only new solutions, but new problems also: one of the issues with the advent of the interweb and the cut-and-paste function is that often students combine the two to devastating effect so that essays, for instance, appear to have been written by Virginia Woolf; which, indeed, they have been.

Analogue note-taking gives distance: a further prism or sieve that refracts the information and the manner in which it is expressed away from merely copying the original. Note-taking is a process through which students can, erm, process (or digest) the material before picking up a laptop. Explicit teaching of the skills of note-taking is at least a partial warning that they should not skip the phase and go direct to writing the essay without having done proper research, resulting in papers that Matt Birkenhauer, who teaches English at Northern Kentucky University, describes in his blog post 'The Lost Art of Note Taking When Writing a Research Paper' as being the kind we all recognise: 'slapdash, lacking in depth or analysis, a patch quilt of different sources that don't go anywhere'.[98][99]

How then should we teach note-taking? Samantha Dhann from the University of Exeter has produced a fairly exhaustive study of note-taking and how to do it that is worth paraphrasing. In it, she outlines that there are two main versions of note-taking: linear and spray-type. It is fashionable in certain circles to promote the spray-type over linear as it is seen to reflect the brain's divergent patterns more accurately than linear forms of note-taking, though I'll leave this to you to decide on your own preference. Where Dhann

---

98 Which could serve quite comfortably as a review of this book.
99 Matt Birkenhauer, 'The Lost Art of Note Taking When Writing a Research Paper' (2011). Available at http://www.facultyfocus.com/articles/teaching-and-learning/the-lost-art-of-note-taking-when-writing-a-research-paper/ (accessed 22 May 2013).

is interesting is in summarising the thought processes that a student might go through to decide whether something said is worthy of being taken down in note form:

> It is important to determine which pieces of information in a lecture or reading are important and which pieces are not. The best way to do this is to be critical when you read or listen. Ask yourself if the information you're hearing is IMPORTANT, RELEVANT, and CREDIBLE. In other words, does the information demonstrate a major point, does it relate to the subject matter, and is it believable or supported?[100]

She goes on to suggest that a note-taker should also be able to distinguish between fact, opinion and example, suggesting that where a teacher has given an example it is better not to copy this down verbatim; it can be a more interesting and cognitively useful process to think of and write down your own examples (it may be that a key would be of use here: F (fact), O (opinion) or E (example)). Her most interesting assertion is in the form of a question: a student taking notes should be in possession of a quest to answer the following question: where are the gaps?

She then goes on to looking at the SQ3R (Survey, Question, Read, Recall and Review) approach to taking notes from a text, which was devised by Derek Rowntree[101] and is a systematic reading strategy for approaching research tasks with texts actively and reflectively:

- Survey: this is where you read the text to locate what it is about. It will be at this stage that you will be able to make a snap decision as to whether you are reading the right text.

---

100 Samantha Dhann, 'Note Taking Skills – From Lectures and Readings' (2001). Available at http://education.exeter.ac.uk/dll/studyskills/note_taking_skills.htm (accessed 22 May 2013).
101 Derek Rowntree, *Learn How to Study: A Programmed Introduction to Better Study Techniques* (London, Mcdonald, 1970).

- Question: this is where you locate or outline the questions that you want the text to answer for you. This is vital stage if you want your research to be as effective as it might be.

- Read: as a direct response to the questions you have outlined that you want answered you now attempt to locate these answers. It is suggested that you read critically, judging whether what you are reading makes the right connections with your purpose in reading the text.

- Recall: either this is the stage at which you take notes (though I'd suggest that you do so concurrently as you are reading) or this is the stage that you close the book and attempt to recall what you have read through the process of either reading your notes or asking yourself the simple question, 'Did I learn the answers to the questions I wanted answered?'

- Review: open the text again. Check that you haven't missed anything. Supplement your notes if you are able.

A young correspondent of mine,[102] an assistant head teacher called Caroline Creaby, who is also a doctoral student, has a technique that she uses for her doctoral studies, but has also employed with her students and which she says forces them to think as they read rather than being purely passive vessels: 'Get students to split a page in three, drawing one line about 70% of the way down the page, and the other 90% down the page. The top section (70%) should be labelled "notes" and they can write whatever they like in whatever format. Next section (20%) is for a 25 word summary of the notes thus far. And the final section (10%) is for 5 key words (not continuous prose).'[103]

---

102 This was meant to sound upsettingly creepy.
103 Caroline Creaby, Personal Communication 1st May 2013

The issue here, in that this is a book about plenaries, is how we transform note-taking into a plenary task. (As well, perhaps, as the fact that note-taking implies the students will have been in receipt of a lecture from Sir or Miss, and lectures are held by the pedagogic orthodoxy to be morally reprehensible.) But we could plausibly give students an analogue research task to do based around the SQ3R method above, and have them either copy up their notes as a plenary task or discuss them in some 'experimental' grouping strategy. Alternatively, we might ask them to copy up their notes as a homework task.

8. REHEARSING AND MEMORISING

Rehearsing and memorising	Memorisation of material by overt or covert strategies	Writing down a mathematics formula until it is remembered

Source: John Hattie, *Visible Learning: A Synthesis of over 800 Meta-Analyses Relating to Achievement* (Abingdon: Routledge, 2009), Table 9.5, at 190.

As any parent with primary age children will tell you, while helping their kids learn spellings through the look–say–cover–write–check technique, repetition works. Though it seems somewhat grandiose to call writing down a mathematical formula until it is remembered a strategy, if it works, it works.

There are more complex memory strategies than just repeating the same action and many of these come under the title of meta-memory strategies.

META-MEMORY STRATEGIES

There's an errant genius called Andy Salmon who's made it his life's work to get down to some serious 'linking', which is a series of means through which you remember things. It's an odd way to make a living, but Andy, who also goes by the name of Sir Linkalot (and who can be found on www.thinkalink. co.uk), whilst undoubtedly bordering on the obsessive, is also undeniably brilliant at remembering things. His book *Think of a Link: How to Remember Absolutely Everything*[104] has an introduction in which he goes through the key ways of remembering: rhyming, acronyms, stories and humour/puns.

Rhyming Links

Andy's example is related to remembering the date of the gunpowder plot, (which was 1605), and who the king was at the time. He informs you that 1605 can also be the twenty-four hour clock time for five past four, and then comes up with the rhyming link:

There was a bang at the door

At five past four

King James the Scot

Didn't like flames a lot.[105]

Invent your own!

Acrostic Links

· **For spelling**: Big Elephants Can 'Ardly Understand Sausage Eaters. You get the point. It's not difficult, but it can be fun if you avoid the obvious.

---

104 Andy Salmon, *Think of a Link: How to Remember Absolutely Everything* (Maidstone: Bonkers Books, 2011).
105 Salmon, *Think of a Link*, 9.

'Runny Runny Help … Oops'[106] is a very good way of remembering how to spell the difficult bit in the word diarrhoea, for instance. A plenary that featured a section in which acrostics were used for spelling key terms might be effective in ensuring students are able to write them accurately.

- **For sequences**: Andy's solution to remembering the order of the planets in the solar system is 'My Very Enormous Monster Just Sucked Up Neptune'.[107] You can see how anything in which an order must be learnt is possible through this technique.

Story Links

This technique is actually as old as the hills, and is related to the Roman method of loci, which is somewhat amusingly also known as the rather more grand 'memory palace'. Legend has it that it all came about when a banquet in ancient times was somewhat ruined by the roof catching fire and killing most of the guests. Bummer. The host was then asked to identify who exactly the burned remnants of people used to be before they'd been turned into charcoal, and the clever feller remembered them by recalling who was sitting at which place around the table. 'Well, the twisted piece of carbon fibre contorted into a squirming tableau of agony directly to my left is Dennis …' As a result of this silly little story, whenever Cicero and his mates wanted to remember something (particularly in a specific order) they would allocate places or locations to them. There's science behind why this method works – and it does work: some poor autistic and entirely friendless sap is

---

106 Salmon, *Think of a Link*, 22.

107 Salmon, *Think of a Link*, 11. (Oh, and Pluto's not a planet any more. But he's still Micky Mouse's dog.)

reported as having used it to memorise pi to 65,536 digits[108] – but what your students need to know about the loci method is that they undertake a journey in their heads and place objects at various points of the journey.

> When desiring to remember a set of items the subject literally 'walks' through these loci and commits an item to each one by forming an image between the item and any distinguishing feature of that locus. Retrieval of items is achieved by 'walking' through the loci, allowing the latter to activate the desired items.[109]

This journey can be through a building with which you are familiar – a super-market, a street or, particularly, your own home. The key is that it has to be somewhere that you know well: it might be your journey to school or your nan's boudoir.

You can, of course, simply use the loci method, but a derivation of this that comes with the recommendation of Sir Linkalot is the production of brief narratives featuring silly plays on words. When Sir Linkalot wants to remember that Everest is in Nepal and was first climbed by Hillary and Tenzing, he invents the following pointless narrative:

> I need to Everest as I've a Nepalling stitch and my legs are Tenzing up. This mountain is a little more Hillary than I envisaged.[110]

I didn't get it first time either. Think about it. 'Everest' sounds like 'have a rest'. 'A Nepalling' sounds like 'an appalling'. Sure, the puns are pure fromage, and it feels like a technique for five-year-olds, but you might just be teaching five-year-olds. If you are teaching older kids, then you can elevate the

---

108 Good work feller!
109 John O'Keefe and Lynn Nadel, *The Hippocampus as a Cognitive Map* (New York: Oxford University Press, 1978), 389–390.
110 Salmon, *Think of a Link*, 15.

intellectual level by using the technique to remember more complex and serious pieces of information.

Humour Links

Humour links, which Sir Linkalot describes as being 'linking good pun' (which is, I believe, a linking good pun on blinking good fun, though I accept that it is not very punny), are best when they are 'toe-curlingly-cheesy-you-have-to-be-kidding-me jokes'. He then goes on to cite an example: to remember that an aviary is where birds live you could recite the phrase, 'Aviary day I wake up the birds are singing'.[111]

But to create a humour link you must first understand what a pun is. Asking students to come up with puns can be a fruitless activity, as they will sit en masse with an empty piece of paper for ten minutes, which they will hand in at the end with nothing other than their name and the word 'puns' written on it.

HOW DO PUNS WORK?

A woman walks into a bar and asks for a double entendre ... So the barman gives her one.[112]

This section is, to a certain extent, obviously just an excuse to share with you a series of puns, but if we go back to the objectives, it is also so that you can

---

111 Salmon, *Think of a Link*, 21.
112 Thanks to Glen McLachlan for this joke.

teach students how puns work in order that they may use them to create humour links to memorise the knowledge they have acquired in the lesson.

It was the pun, rather than sarcasm, that Samuel Johnson termed the lowest form of humour. The pun is merely a device that exploits the fact that words have more than one meaning. An ejaculation during intercourse, which whilst correct, alludes to something else entirely but in doing so makes us snigger like guilty, dirty schoolboys. William Safire of the *New York Times* continues the sexual metaphor with his claim that 'A pun is to wordplay what dominatrix sex is to foreplay – a stinging whip that elicits groans of guilty pleasure'.[113]

Puns separate into homophonic puns, in which the sounds of words can get confused (the kind of pun that is its own reword, and is very much the lesser of two weevils), and homographic puns, which exploit the fact that radically different meanings can be attributed to the same spelling. Such as the one where the man walks into a bar, and it was a metal bar, so he really hurt himself because metal is hard and isn't a very good thing to walk into if you can possibly avoid it. Maybe he wasn't looking where he was going. Or something.

How does a pun differ from double entendre? It doesn't really. (Though one might argue that if it's rude enough to be a double entendre, it may be too rude even for the classroom in which students will give you a warm hand on your entrance.)

So, now students know about puns they can construct humorous, punning links with which to memorise information as a plenary task. Share them. Laugh like drugged up hyenas. Consider retirement.

---

113 William Safire, 'Conundrum Beat' (2005). Available at http://www.nytimes.com/2005/10/23/magazine/23onlanguage.html?_r=0 (accessed 22 May 2013).

9. GOAL-SETTING/PLANNING

Goal-setting/ planning	Setting of educational goals or planning of sub-goals and planning for sequencing, timing and completing activities related to those goals

Source: John Hattie, *Visible Learning: A Synthesis of over 800 Meta-Analyses Relating to Achievement* (Abingdon: Routledge, 2009), Table 9.5, at 190.

These are no more or no less than the metacognitive strategies outlined on page 100–103, and can easily be translated into a proforma that can be used by your students to help them with planning, monitoring and regulation. At the end of the lesson ask students to fill out the following form and allow that form to guide them through a research task they have set themselves.

Metacognitive Strategy Proforma – Research Homework	
Identify the thing about this lesson that you think you need to know more about	
How are you going to find out more about it at home? List three ways	

Once you have found out what you needed to know how are you going to demonstrate that new understanding in your homework? What task will you choose?	
What are the steps you will take once you have found out in order to demonstrate your new understanding?	
When are you going to do this? How long will you spend on it?	
How will you tell that you are happy with your homework? What criteria will you have to fulfil to satisfy yourself and your teacher that you have performed well on this task?	

10. REVIEWING RECORDS

Reviewing records	Efforts to reread notes, tests or textbooks to prepare for class or further testing	Reviewing class text-book before going to lecture

Source: John Hattie, *Visible Learning: A Synthesis of over 800 Meta-Analyses Relating to Achievement* (Abingdon: Routledge, 2009), Table 9.5, at 190.

You don't need my help on this one. Revision is of value. Students should schedule it.

11. SELF-MONITORING

Self-monitoring	Observing and tracking one's own performance and actions, often recording them	Keeping records of study output

Source: John Hattie, *Visible Learning: A Synthesis of over 800 Meta-Analyses Relating to Achievement* (Abingdon: Routledge, 2009), Table 9.5, at 190.

As an academic concept, self-monitoring is actually the study of how we operate socially, in terms of how we modify our behaviour according to the cues we receive from others. A high self-monitor would be sensitive to the reactions of others, and will adjust their behaviour to obtain positive reactions in others. Low self-monitors don't give a monkey's what other people think of them; they behave as they like and if they see something they want they just take it; and good luck to them. (At least they are not living under the perpetual angst of wearing the people-pleasing disguise of conformity.)

If we relocate the concept to individual academic study, then self-monitoring is clearly about modifying your behaviour to maximise your performance in class. The best work on this comes from the United States, and the most influential piece of pedagogy – which is predominantly related to reading comprehension strategies – is the Stop, Ask, Fix technique, or the Stop-Think strategy originated by Sue Mowery.[114]

---

114 Available at http://teacher.scholastic.com/reading/bestpractices/comprehension/stopaskfix-checklist.pdf (accessed 22 May 2013).

One of the seminal texts in the scintillating area of self-monitoring is Jeffrey Wilhelm's *Navigating Meaning: Using Think-Alouds to Help Readers Monitor Comprehension*. He comes up with a detailed self-monitoring strategy for students to use while they are reading to ensure that they comprehend the text they are reading, which he calls 'think-alouds'. Recall, as you are reading, that these steps are based on a reading comprehension programme, and ponder how the process might be related to the plenary.

In the section of Wilhelm's book titled 'From Modeling to Students' Independent Use: Basic Steps' it lists four steps to take to improve students' comprehension facilities:[115]

1 **Teacher does/students watch**

Wilhelm models a variety of strategies then puts them in the form of a flow diagram. He then posts the flow chart up on one or several walls in the classroom.

2 **Teacher does/students help**

He then reads a further text and takes students through the steps outlined in the flow diagram, but this time it is a collaborative task shared by students and teacher. The students prompt the teacher, telling him or her what they must do next.

3 **Students do/teacher helps**

He then puts them into groups and asks them to perform the function in this new collaborative environment, supporting while they do so, asking them to pause and ask themselves if what they are reading

---

115 Jeffrey D. Wilhelm, *Improving Comprehension with Think-Aloud Strategies* (Jefferson City, MO: Scholastic Professional Books, 2001), 97.

makes sense. If it isn't making sense they are asked to use basic strategies such as re-reading, reading ahead or skipping/filling in words.

4   Students do/teacher helps

Here students might carry out the 'self' bit of self-monitoring and will work individually. Wilhelm suggests giving them the Stop, Ask, Fix checklist designed by Sue Mowery.

Wilhelm translates this process to the plenary as a set diary task during the lesson (or preferably over a series of lessons) in which students monitor their lesson behaviours with reference to their own pre-existing metacognitive knowledge. From then on, over the space of a good, long agglomeration of many ten-minute sessions, they produce their own flow-chart of lesson performance and the metacognitive strategies they might best employ to properly self-regulate during lessons.

This sounds a very difficult thing to pull off. However, remembering that Hattie states that metacognition has an effect size second only to feedback, then this is actually of potentially serious value to students: a flow chart stuck to the inside front cover of their books that reminds them what to do in lessons in order to monitor their own performance and to remind them of strategies that they find helpful in this regard.

12. TASK STRATEGIES

Task strategies	Analysing tasks and identifying specific, advantageous methods for learning	Creating mnemonics to remember facts

Source: John Hattie, *Visible Learning: A Synthesis of over 800 Meta-Analyses Relating to Achievement* (Abingdon: Routledge, 2009), Table 9.5, at 190.

On first sight, the presence of mnemonics as the example here jars: one wonders how on earth you might use task strategies as a plenary function, as clearly they appear to be of use prior to a task. However, if one locates the intent of the plenary as a task, the function of which is to lodge the lesson's content in the head of the student, then they might easily be asked this question and then pick from a range of plenary functions outlined to them as potential options (which might reasonably include mnemonics). Indeed, we might even be able to give them a proforma from which they can select their own task strategies, which might resemble rather closely an abridged contents list from this very book.

Potential task strategy for learning the information from the lesson
Identify one question you are left with, two concepts you understand that you didn't know before and three new pieces of vocabulary you now know along with what they mean.
Do something abstract with the information. You may decide to draw it, write a poem or song about it, imagine it as a character and ask it questions.
Identify what is the exact opposite to the learning. Identify a tangent to the learning. Represent this diagrammatically.
Draw a frozen picture of the learning. Draw a mime of it.
Identify the key pieces of vocabulary from the lesson and tell a story featuring each of these pieces of vocabulary.
Find out whether your parents are daft. Create a quiz on the learning for them. Devise ten questions.
Create a passage about the learning from the lesson that has a number of deliberate errors. Make them difficult to spot – see if your teacher can find them.
See if you can create a Venn diagram, Euler diagram, Carroll diagram, Ishikawa diagram or mind map with the learning.
Devise yourself a schedule for the four times you are going to recall this information to lodge it in your head. Write this down in your planner.

Identify separately the social, emotional, subject-orientated and metacognitive aspects of the lesson's learning.

Analyse your own performance in this lesson in terms of what you know about goal orientation theory.

Devise questions that you will use as a writing frame to evaluate the effectiveness of this lesson in terms of your learning.

Take the materials you have been provided in this lesson and somehow rearrange them: re-sequencing, highlighting, re-writing.

Create a passage in which you relate the content of the lesson to your dreams and your fears. Do not be glib here. Is there any way you can relate the content of this lesson to your dreams? How might not learning the lesson contribute to your fears? What could go wrong in your life if you do not know the information you have learnt today?

See if you can create a rich visual image related to the learning. Draw it. Or write a film script in which this image features.

Write a series of steps for a younger child to learn this information. Find a younger child and teach them it.

List a series of interesting places the information from this lesson might lead you in terms of further study. Then list three places or people from whom you might find this information out.

Assess your performance in this lesson in terms of learning and then share your assessment with someone else.

Write notes on the lesson.
Write a diary entry in your metacognitive diary.[116]
Write down the most important information from the lesson ten times.
Create a rhyming link.
Create an acrostic link.
Create a story link using the method of loci.
Create a punning link with the information.

116 Is this too leftfield an idea? Or are we in very interesting territory here – students keeping a metacognitive diary as a weekly homework task?

14. TIME MANAGEMENT

Time management	Estimating and budgeting use of time	Scheduling daily studying and homework time

Source: John Hattie, *Visible Learning: A Synthesis of over 800 Meta-Analyses Relating to Achievement* (Abingdon: Routledge, 2009), Table 9.5, at 190.

Firstly, if you are wondering what happened to (13), you've already had it: it was Imagery and was combined with (3), Self-Consequences.

Unfortunately, regarding time management, I, erm didn't manage it. And if you can briefly imagine the relief you might experience if you had stupidly agreed to write a book on the most boring aspect of teaching, and then spent six long months grappling with it every long, long evening, desperately using every piece of metacognitive knowledge you had to keep driving it forward to a conclusion that looked like it would never happen, then you'll forgive me. I really don't have the time.

POTENTIALLY USEFUL RESOURCES FOR SPODS

COGNITIVE-METACOGNITIVE FRAMEWORK

Garofalo and Lester, 'Metacognition, Cognitive Monitoring and Mathematical Performance'.

MOTIVATED STRATEGIES FOR LEARNING QUESTIONNAIRE

Paul R. Pintrich and Elisabeth V. De Groot, 'Motivational and Self-Regulated Learning Components of Classroom Academic Performance, *Journal of Educational Psychology* 82(1) (1990): 33–40.

FLOW CHART OF COMPREHENSION-MONITORING BEHAVIOURS

Available at http://teacher.scholastic.com/reading/bestpractices/comprehension/flowchartofbehavior.pdf (accessed 22 May 2013)

STOP, ASK, FIX STUDENT CHECKLIST

Available at http://teacher.scholastic.com/reading/bestpractices/comprehension/stopaskfixchecklist.pdf (accessed 22 May 2013).

VISUALISATION CHECKLIST FOR READING COMPREHENSION

Available at http://www.scholastic.com/teachers/article/collateral_resources/pdf/r/reading_bestpractices_comprehension_visualization.pdf (accessed 22 May 2013).

BIBLIOGRAPHY

Ames, Carol (1992) 'Classrooms: Goals, Structures and Student Motivation', *Journal of Educational Psychology* 84(3): 261–271.

Anderson, John R., Reder, Lynne M. and Simon, Herbert A. (1996) 'Situated Learning and Education', *Educational Researcher* 25(4): 5–11.

Azevedo, Roger and Cromley, Jennifer G. (2004) 'Does Training on Self-Regulated Learning Facilitate Students' Learning with Hypermedia?' *Journal of Educational Psychology* 96(3): 523–535.

Bartle, Keven (2013) 'The Myth of Progress within Lessons'. Available at http://dailygenius. wordpress.com/2013/02/12/the-myth-of-progress-within-lessons/ (accessed 22 May 2013).

Beadle, Phil (2007) 'Shhh, Let's Not Tell the Kids What We're Trying To Do'. Available at http://www.guardian.co.uk/education/2007/jan/16/schools.uk1 (accessed 22 May 2013).

Beadle, Phil (2008) *Could Do Better! Help Your Kid Shine At School*. London: Corgi.

Beadle, Phil (2010) *How to Teach*. Carmarthen: Crown House.

Beadle, Phil (2011) *Dancing about Architecture: A Little Book of Creativity*. Carmarthen: Crown House.

Beadle, Phil (2012) 'High Scores Come At a Higher Cost'. Available at http://www.smh.com.au/opinion/politics/high-scores-come-at-a-higher-cost-20120729-2365e.html#ixzz2A9cUMiEK (accessed 22 May 2013).

Birkenhauer, Matt (2011) 'The Lost Art of Note Taking When Writing a Research Paper'. Available at http://www.facultyfocus.com/articles/teaching-and-learning/the-lost-art-of-note-taking-when-writing-a-research-paper/ (accessed 22 May 2013).

Black, Paul, Harrison, Christine, Lee, Clare, Marshall, Bethan and Wiliam, Dylan (1990) *Working Inside the Black Box: Assessment for Learning in the Classroom*. Glasgow: Letts.

Black, Paul and Wiliam, Dylan (1990) *Inside the Black Box: Raising Standards through Classroom Assessment*. London: GL Assessment.

Broudy, Harry S. (1987) 'The Role of Imagery in Learning', Occasional Paper 1. Los Angeles, CA: Getty Center for Education in the Arts.

Bull, Britta L. and Wittrock, Merlin C. (1973) 'Imagery in the Learning of Verbal Definitions', *British Journal of Educational Psychology* 43(3): 289–293.

Chesterton, G. K. (2004) *Orthodoxy*. Mineola, NY: Dover.

Christoddou, Daisy (2013) *Seven Myths about Education*. London: The Curriculum Centre.

Cox, David (2012) 'How Your Brain Likes To Be Treated at Revision Time'. Available at http://www.guardian.co.uk/education/mortarboard/2012/nov/06/how-your-brain-likes-to-revise (accessed 22 May 2013).

DeShon, Richard P. and Gillespie, Jennifer Z. (2005) 'A Motivated Action Theory Account of Goal Orientation', *Journal of Applied Psychology* 90(6): 1096–1127.

Dhann, Samantha (2001) 'Note Taking Skills – From Lectures and Readings'. Available at http://education.exeter.ac.uk/dll/studyskills/note_taking_skills.htm (accessed 22 May 2013).

Dix, Paul (2011) 'Stop Thinking That Your Objectives Interest Me'. Available at http://www.pivotaleducation.com/stop-thinking-that-your-objectives-interest-me/ (accessed 22 May 2013).

Flavell, John H. (1976) 'Metacognitive Aspects of Problem Solving', in Lauren B. Resnick (ed.), *The Nature of Intelligence*. Hillsdale, NJ: Erlbaum, pp. 231–236.

Flavell, John H. (1979) 'Metacognition and Cognitive Monitoring: A New Area of Cognitive/Developmental Inquiry', *American Psychologist* 34(10): 906–911.

Foote, Allison L. and Crystal, Jonathon D. (2007) 'Metacognition in the Rat', *Current Biology* 17(6): 551–555.

Garofalo, Joe and Lester, Frank K. (1985) 'Metacognition, Cognitive Monitoring and Mathematical Performance', *Journal for Research in Mathematics Education* 16: 163–176.

Goleman, Daniel (1995) *Emotional Intelligence: Why It Can Matter More Than IQ*. London: Bloomsbury.

Halpern, Diane F. (1998) 'Teaching Critical Thinking for Transfer across Domains: Dispositions, Skills, Structure Training and Metacognitive Monitoring', *American Psychologist* 53(4): 449–455.

Hattie, John (2009) *Visible Learning: A Synthesis of over 800 Meta-Analyses Relating to Achievement*. Abingdon: Routledge.

Hattie, John (2012) *Visible Learning for Teachers: Maximising Impact on Learning*. Abingdon: Routledge.

Higgins, Steve, Katsipataki, Maria, Kokotsaki, Dimitra, Coleman, Robbie, Major, Lee Elliot and Coe, Rob (2013) *The Sutton Trust – Education Endowment Foundation Teaching and Learning Toolkit*. London: Education Endowment Foundation.

Huang, Jeff J. S., Yang, Stephen J. H., Chiang, Poky Y. F. and Tzeng, Luis S. Y. (2012) 'Building an E-Portfolio Learning Model: Goal Orientation and Metacognitive Strategies', *Knowledge Management & E-Learning: An International Journal* 4(1): 16–36.

Hughes, Carolyn (1997) 'Self-Instruction', in Martin Agran (ed.), *Student-Directed Learning: Teaching Self-Determination Skills*. Detroit, MI: Brooks/Cole, pp. 144–170.

Kaplan, Avi and Maehr, Martin L. (2007) 'The Contributions and Prospects of Goal Orientation Theory', *Educational Psychology Review* 19(2): 141–184.

Lavery, Lynn (2008) 'Self-Regulated Learning for Academic Success: An Evaluation of Instructional Techniques', unpublished PhD thesis, University of Auckland.

Lawton, Fiona (2004) 'Using the Plenary to Develop Reflective and Critical Thinking and to Enhance Metacognitive Awareness: Student Teachers' Perceptions and School-Based Experiences of the Daily Mathematics Lesson Plenary', *Proceedings of the British Society for Research into Learning Mathematics* 24(2): 63–67.

Lovett, Marsha C. (2008) 'Teaching Metacognition'. Presentation to the Educause Learning Initiative Annual Meeting, 29 January.

Mead, Darren (2010) 'Metacognitive Wrappers'. Available at http://Pedagogicalpurposes. blogspot.co.uk/2010/11/metacognitive-wrappers.html (accessed 22 May 2013).

Metcalfe, Janet and Shimamura, Arthur P. (1994) *Metacognition: Knowing about Knowing*. Cambridge, MA: MIT Press.

Ofsted (2001) *The National Literacy Strategy: The Third Year*. Ref: 332. London: Ofsted. Available at: http://www.ofsted.gov.uk/resources/national-literacy-strategy-third-year (accessed 22 May 2013).

Ofsted (2002) *The Key Stage 3 Strategy: Evaluation of the First Year of the Pilot*. Ref: 349. London: Ofsted. Available at: http://dera.ioe.ac.uk/16531/ (accessed 22 May 2013).

Ofsted (2012) *Moving English Forward*. Ref: 110118. London: Ofsted. Available at: http://www. ofsted.gov.uk/resources/moving-english-forward (accessed 22 May 2013).

O'Keefe, John and Nadel, Lynn (1978) *The Hippocampus as a Cognitive Map*. New York: Oxford University Press.

Paivio, Allan (1971) *Imagery and Verbal Processes*. New York: Holt, Rinehart, and Winston.

Petty, Geoff (2002) '25 Ways for Teaching without Talking: Presenting Students with New Material in Theory Lessons'. Available at http://geoffpetty.com/for-team-leaders/downloads/ (accessed 22 May 2013).

Pintrich Paul R. and De Groot, Elisabeth V. (1990) 'Motivational and Self-Regulated Learning Components of Classroom Academic Performance', *Journal of Educational Psychology* 82(1): 33–40.

Rowntree Derek (1970) *Learn How to Study: A Programmed Introduction to Better Study Techniques*. London: Mcdonald.

Safire, William (2005) 'Conundrum Beat'. Available at http://www.nytimes.com/2005/10/23/ magazine/23onlanguage.html?_r=0 (accessed 22 May 2013).

Salmon, Andy (2011) *Think of a Link: How to Remember Absolutely Everything*. Maidstone: Bonkers Books.

Smith, Jim (2012) *Whole School Progress the Lazy Way: Follow Me I'm Right Behind You*. Carmarthen: Crown House.

Utman, Christopher H. (1997) 'Performance Effects of Motivational States: A Meta-Analysis', *Personality and Social Psychology Review* 1: 170–182.

Vanderstoep, Scott W. and Pintrich, Paul R. (1996) 'Disciplinary Differences in Self-Regulated Learning in College Students', *Contemporary Educational Psychology* 21(4): 345–362.

Veenman, Marcel V. J., Van Hout-Wolters, Bernadette H. A. M. and Afflerbach, Peter (2006) 'Metacognition and Learning: Conceptual and Methodological Considerations', *Metacognition & Learning* 1: 3–14.

Wehmeyer, Michael L. (2006) 'Self-Instruction'. Available at http://www.dps.missouri.edu/resources/MoreThanAJob/Supports/Supports%202/02%20Self-Instruction.htm (accessed 22 May 2013).

Wehmeyer, Michael L., Agran, Martin and Hughes, Carolyn (1998) 'Teaching Self-Instruction Skills', in *eidem*, *Teaching Self-Determination to Students with Disabilities: Basic Skills for Successful Transition*. Baltimore, MD: Paul H. Brookes, pp. 157–183.

Wilhelm, Jeffrey D. (2001) *Navigating Meaning: Improving Comprehension with Think-Aloud Strategies*. Jefferson City, MO: Scholastic Professional Books.

Young, Bradley W. and Starkes, Janet L. (2006) 'Coaches' Perceptions of Non-Regulated Training Behaviors in Competitive Swimmers', *International Journal of Sports Science and Coaching* 1: 53–68.

INDEX

Swartz, Aaron 113
Swimming 104–105

T

Twitter 93
Tzeng, Luis 91

U

Utman, Christopher 90

V

Venn diagrams 71, 151

W

Warburton, Simon 42
Wehmeyer, Michael 125, 126
Wilhelm, Jeffrey 148–149
Wiliam, Dylan 23, 24, 25
Wittrock, Merlin 122–123

Y

Yang, Stephen 91
Young, Bradley W. 105

HOW TO TEACH

Semantics, stanzas and semi colons ...

Literacy
across the curriculum

PHIL BEADLE

ISBN 978-178135128-4

The 'How to Teach' series covers every element of classroom practice
in a highly practical, but wildly irreverent, manner.

independentthinkingpress.com

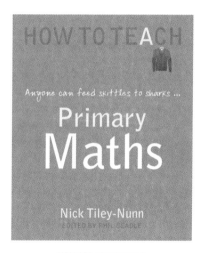

ISBN 978-178135135-2

The 'How to Teach' series covers every element of classroom practice
in a highly practical, but wildly irreverent, manner.

independentthinkingpress.com

PHIL BEADLE

How to teach

provokes, at times shocks, but above all teaches   controversial
readable, hugely readable   necessary, hugely necessary   irreverent
hip, sharp, sussed, funny and extremely practical   hilarious
a scintillating, pedagogical romp   intoxicating, deeply wise
laugh-out-loud, embarass-yourself-in-public funny

ISBN 978-184590393-0

The 'How to Teach' series covers every element of classroom practice
in a highly practical, but wildly irreverent, manner.

independentthinkingpress.com